Praise

"Ian McCoog's new book is a highly original and deeply reflective take on the nature of leadership. Both an essential primer on the history and theory of the field and a compelling collection of personal stories of leaders in action, *Leadership Bites* is entertaining, wise, and inspirational. Highly recommended!"

—Damian Tarnopolsky, author of *Every Night I Dream I'm a Monk, Every Night I Dream I'm a Monster*

"Using his expert research skills, Dr. Ian McCoog writes about the important yet difficult task of being a leader. He provides fascinating, absorbing, and inspiring anecdotes that will help any emerging leader navigate their new role."

—Kayla Branstetter, author of *Don't Be an Athena*

"Leadership is complex. In *Leadership Bites,* Ian McCoog has culled important and powerful nuggets from generations of leadership theories and models, highlighting both the overlap and divergence of the array of leadership approaches and characteristics. The stories he shares vividly illustrate each leadership approach in a way that engages the brain and touches the heart."

—Paul Reinert, associate professor of educational leadership at Wilkes University

Leadership Bites

Leadership Bites

An Approachable Handbook for Emerging Leaders

Ian J. McCoog

Montpelier, VT

Leadership Bites ©2024 Ian J. McCoog

Release date: January 28, 2025

All Rights Reserved

Printed in the USA.

Published by Rootstock Publishing,
an imprint of Ziggy Media LLC
info@rootstockpublishing.com
www.rootstockpublishing.com

Paperback ISBN: 978-1-57869-184-5
eBook ISBN: 978-1-57869-185-2

Library of Congress Control Number: 2024923926

Cover and book design by Eddie Vincent, ENC Graphic Services.
Cover photograph: Shutterstock
Charts and other interior photographs provided by the author.

Author photo by Katie McCoog.

For permissions or to schedule a reading, contact the author at
mccoogi@yahoo.com

Contents

Foreword xi
Introduction xv
    What Is Leadership? xv
    The Power of Stories xviii
Chapter 1. Early Theories 1
    You Have to Start Somewhere 3
Chapter 2. Leadership Continuum: Tannenbaum and Schmidt 7
    "I Taught Jack That" 9
Chapter 3. Bases of Power: French and Raven 13
    The Tortoise and the Hare 17
Chapter 4. The Michigan and Ohio State Leadership Studies 21
    Crossing Out the M's 24
Chapter 5. Theories X and Y: McGregor 28
    Theory Z: Ouchi 29
    Regular Hours? 30
Chapter 6. Contingency Model: Fiedler 35
    The 10K Runner 37
Chapter 7. Stages of Group Development: Tuckman .. 40
    Learning Leaves, the Story Stays 43
Chapter 8. Circle of Competence: Buffett and Munger 47
    Bound for Cooperstown 50
Chapter 9. Cognitive Load Theory: Sweller 54
    Decisions, Decisions 58
Chapter 10. Situational Leadership: Hersey and Blanchard .. 62
    Ahhh . . . Spring 65
Chapter 11. Four Frame Model: Bolman and Deal 70
    Structural: The Toolbox 71

Human Resources: The Left Fielder 73
Political: The Gloater 75
Symbolic: The Town 77

Chapter 12. Transactional and Transformational Leadership: Bass 79
Call Me "Bob" 80

Chapter 13. Appreciative Inquiry: Cooperrider and Srivastva . 85
What Would You Do if You Weren't Afraid? 88

Chapter 14. The Leadership Challenge: Kouzes and Posner . 92
The Five Practices and the Ten Commitments 94

Chapter 15. Adaptive Leadership: Heifetz, Linsky, and Grashow 97
Winning and Losing 100

Chapter 16. Resonant Leadership: Goleman, Boyatzis, and McKee 104
Memory of the Present 107

Chapter 17. Quiet Leadership: Rock 111
The Orchestra and the ER 113

Chapter 18. Resilient Leadership: Duggan, Moyer, and Theurer 119
Flush It! 123

Chapter 19. Vulnerable Leadership: Morgan 127
Part 1: The Magic Shop 129
Part 2: Some Old Cardboard 133

Conclusion: *Lakeside* 136
Endnotes 139
Acknowledgments 144
About the Author 147
Bibliography 148

To the memory of Roy A. Montalvan,
who I never met but whose story started it all.

Foreword

by Thomas J. Starmack, EdD, author of *Organizational Behavior: A New Three Dimensional Leadership Paradigm*, professor of educational leadership at the Commonwealth University of Pennsylvania, and chief consultant at FLEX Consulting, LLC.

There are hundreds of books and publications on leadership spanning business, medicine, government, and education. Often authors will interchange the terms of administration, management, and leadership. A strong argument can be made that leadership requires much more than the other two. Managing a schedule, routine, or process can be interpreted as overseeing the implementation and therefore, success. The same can be said for administering a program or an event. Reaching the pinnacle of being a leader requires one critical ingredient, followers. Can a manager or administrator truly be coined a leader without followers?

"Administrator" and "manager" are titles or positions given to a person, whereas, "leader" is earned through trust, actions, credibility, vision, integrity, authenticity, transparency, and people's willingness to follow the path forward. One must understand that programs are managed; people are led. Effective leaders not only have knowledge and skills to garner followers, but they also understand the complexities of the organization within which they operate with a high level of situational awareness to employ the "right" approach at the appropriate time. Leaders know what type and how much power to unleash given a certain situation. Leaders know their people's strengths, have the "right" people in the "right" places to do the "right" things, and create teams that can be synergetic. Leadership knows no role; leaders exist at every level of every organization.

Let's not confuse followership with compliance. Gaining insights to different styles and approaches to leadership enhances one's ability to harness followers. If a supervisor directs an employee to complete a task and the employee does so without any grievances, one cannot assume they are following, rather completing the task so as not to be insubordinate. True followers have a deeper heartfelt or internal belief that is closely aligned with the leader. There are many examples of this throughout history and professions of leaders championing good and not-so-good causes. People as disparate as Gandhi, Taylor Swift, or Rosa Parks have asserted their influence to bring about change. Interestingly, a leader sometimes is simply being a positive role model that causes others to follow the actions to be more like that person. Thus, administrators or managers certainly can earn the title of leader through their behaviors, beliefs, and actions.

Ian McCoog has chosen a unique approach to engaging the reader with various leadership frameworks and tactics where each one has a dynamic story to provide a parallel comparison to leadership in context. The variety of settings and characters helps the reader ponder their point of view as well as the success of the leadership application. Effective leaders anticipate conflict and, of course, most great stories have a level of conflict that needs to be resolved. Learning to approach conflict as an opportunity for a better future can assist in enlisting those individuals who are often difficult to acquire as followers. Through the various stories, the author takes the reader on an eclectic journey spanning different events, venues, countries, and situations to bring relevance to the characteristics of effective leadership. Be employed to read each chapter, and reflect on how one can utilize the knowledge gained to improve your own leadership knowledge and skills as well as increase the number of followers for the greater good.

—Thomas J. Starmack, EdD, 2024

Introduction

What Is Leadership?
I recently attended a workshop during which a colleague asked the presenter what he called a dumb question: "What is leadership?" A scientist through and through, he followed up with, "I mean we all know what it is, but how can we quantify it?" Over coffee later that afternoon, he said to me, "I felt stupid asking but we have to define something in order to measure it." I told him his question wasn't stupid; it was pretty complex. I didn't tell him his query had now stumped two leadership authorities, me and the presenter. I smiled to break the tension that had grown as I considered an answer. My brain raced. I took a sip of coffee to buy myself time.

Leadership is hard to define. It's like art. We know it when we see it. We know it's good when it's good and we know it's bad when it's bad. I gave him a convoluted answer that was more a list of attributes than a definition. "Leadership is consistent behavior in support of others that is reflective in nature, because you must reflect on your actions to be empathetic toward others," I suggested. He looked at me like I had defined love and, you know what, I realized I just might have.

I am a professor working in academic medicine. My research and teaching focus on medical humanities but my true expertise is in leadership studies. I am on the faculty at a medical school but I'm not a doctor (at least not *that* kind of doctor). I like to say, "I'm not a doctor, but I play one at work." In my free time, I write poems, short stories, and speculative history, and have started several novels. Sometimes these works explore themes found in medical humanities, but sometimes they are about folklore or baseball. One consistent thread is that I try to work storytelling into both my scholarship and my work with students.

I always knew I wanted to write a book but I didn't know what it would be about. I thought my dissertation research might beget a book, but it didn't. As it turns out, all I had to do was refine my craft and let the book find me. When I became the go-to person at my school for leadership theory and qualitative data analysis—essentially storytelling—I knew I'd found my book, or rather, it had found me.

I have always been interested in stories. During my first college visits, as a junior in high school interested in studying history, a professor asked me, "Why do you like history?" If you've ever seen the movie *Old School*, you may recall the scene where Will Ferrell's character, Frank the Tank, is surprised to learn he is debating political pundit James Carville. Frank experiences a flash of genius where he gives such a thorough response that Carville has no rebuttal. That is a little like what happened during my college visit. I just started talking about how history is a story and the role of the historian is to interpret, accurately depict, and share that story. The professor just stared, wide-eyed, not quite sure where this sixteen year old's treatise had come from. I got into that college but attended elsewhere.

My first job after college was as a history teacher. Students with even the slightest interest in history seemed to enjoy my classes. Years later I realized it was because I wasn't lecturing; I was telling stories about the past. Storytelling also informs part of my current teaching assignment, leading sessions in our doctoring course on leadership theory. One day after a large group session, a student asked me, "Can't you teach us more things? The way you present material is understandable and it keeps our attention." I was flattered and thanked her. I responded that I would love to teach them "more things" but my limited medical knowledge stopped at practicing empathy with patients and leading a team; it did not include the Krebs Cycle or any immunology whatsoever.

Author Carmine Gallo said, "Storytelling is not something we do. Storytellers are who we are."[1] When I am teaching with stories, I'm not doing anything magical. Neuroscience tells us that storytelling leads to neural coupling, in which the speaker's and the listener's brain rhythms begin to line up, releasing oxytocin. Oxytocin, known as the "love hormone," is vital to bonding. Telling a story might not land you a lover but it does create a temporary bond. These brain responses are believed to be an evolutionary response related to survival through grouping and communication.

Where does leadership come in? This book is a collection of leadership theories curated by me and presented chronologically. Each theory is followed by a short story to illustrate it in a meaningful and hopefully memorable way. For nearly twenty years now, I have been a writer of both academic and creative works; this book has allowed me to combine the two. The straight theory would be dry, so I include stories in the style in which I like to write and tell. In addition, I also include little diagrams that help illustrate the theories, which can be complex concepts for someone new to the field of leadership studies. You are about to read a book about leadership that includes a range of topics such as high jump, old books, crying, power, New England towns, abstract art, teaming, race horses, my family, acapella, and prioritization with a former president.

My goal is to teach you something, not preach my thoughts on leadership or life in general. This handbook is meant to be a reference for those who are new to leadership and looking for an approachable book that will help them in their newfound role. I also hope it can be useful to those who aren't new to leadership but may have never considered the psychology behind it. Some theories are foundational to the field; others are more contemporary. Many are similar, so I aim to highlight how they build upon one another. Some are definitive; some say their application depends on the situation. Other theories say there is no best approach at all. What I present is not one answer but many different ways to think about leading a group.

The Power of Stories
In 2015, Daniel Goleman of Emotional Intelligence fame, published *A Force for Good: The Dalai Lama's Vision for Our World*. Goleman wrote that his Holiness outlined three instructions that we can practice as individuals to make the world around us a better place, the first of which was "manage your inner world."[2]

Stories are how we understand our world. Formulating and telling a story is something just about anyone can do. Five-year-old children tell rambling tales that dip and dive in and out of truth and fantasy. The elderly tell stories full of wisdom and life experience, as long as we take the time to listen. In many ways, I feel like I am a professional story listener and teller. The courses I teach focus on medical humanities, leadership in medicine, and the skills that future physicians need to better connect with patients. I'm more qualified to teach our students from a patient's perspective than a physician's, and that is exactly what makes me valuable to my school.

I learned about the intricacies of academic medicine on the job. My background in educational leadership has refined into a specialty in medical education leadership. The fact that I'm an academic doctor and not a medical doctor at my core is a unique perspective that allows me to work with students on the beautiful art of medicine. I often ask questions like, How will this diagnosis affect the patient's lifestyle? Or, Why is it so hard to stop a bad habit even when you know it is negatively affecting your health? Nevertheless, my most important role is as a listener when I ask my students: What is your story?

Before we go too deep, let's establish the difference between a "story" and a "narrative" as I use the terms: A story is told through a narrative structure. You might think Uncle Billy isn't considering structure when telling a tale around the campfire after a few beers. He's not, but he probably unconsciously follows a narrative structure by virtue of telling a story.

A linear narrative follows a story from beginning to middle to end. Most Hollywood movies are linear narratives. A nonlinear narrative is a story that evolves as pieces come together. A true-crime investigation show is a good example of a nonlinear narrative. The detective uncovers clues that reveal the whole picture.

A viewpoint narrative is told from a single, first-person perspective. These narratives are defined by how the story is presented, as opposed to a particular chronology. A descriptive narrative focuses less on the characters and more on the setting and immersion in the world of the story.[3]

I hope my students gain an understanding of the people around them by listening to each other's stories (for an example of Affiliative leadership—see page 103). I also hope they gain the ability to piece together stories to create an understanding of a larger context (Visionary leadership, page 103). Each puzzle piece reveals a unique portion of the picture. Each unique tree makes up the forest. Are you a corner puzzle piece or a middle? Are you a red pine or an oak? When trying to make sense of a situation, some stories may contribute more than others but each one is important (Democratic leadership, page 103). Reflecting on your own story not only helps you better understand yourself professionally, but it helps you protect yourself by being mindful of triggers and defining boundaries. Leaders are useless to their teams if they don't take care of their own needs.

In my experience teaching and writing, I've found the most important part of storytelling is knowing your own story and feeling comfortable sharing it. I purposefully chose this to be the first "story" coupled with the introduction of this book, and I hope my allusions with the provided page numbers have you thinking about what's coming up.

The only way to be genuine with yourself is through self-reflection. When you know yourself, you know your presuppositions and potential biases. When I meet with students, we often discuss how being honest with yourself opens you up to being more compassionate, patient-centered, community-minded, and interprofessional-focused (Coaching leadership, page 103). These characteristics are some of the hardest skills for physicians to gain. Being comfortable sharing your story is important because, although it may make you feel vulnerable, it also helps to build trust. An environment where your team and colleagues understand each other's backgrounds and do not pass judgment surpasses an organization with a mere collegial community.

> "If you are going to share widely—make sure you're sharing from your scars and not your open wounds."
> —Nadia Bolz-Weber

At the beginning of this story, I cited the first instruction from the Dalai Lama regarding one's inner world. His second instruction is, "Turn toward others with empathy and compassion." Number three is, "Act for the greater good." If you understand yourself, you'll better understand those you serve.

Chapter 1

Early Theories

"Thanks to my leadership skills—cowering, running, and pulling a skedaddle—we are safe..."

—Captain Smek

Some of the earliest ideas of what makes a good leader were neither inclusive nor evidence-based, and have not stood the test of time. In the mid-1800s, Thomas Carlyle wrote about heroism, proposing that history was simply the biography of great men. This evolved into his proposed Great Man Theory which held in high regard figures like Napoleon, Shakespeare, and George Washington. Carlyle's theory assumed that leaders were born with innate traits that came to the surface when the opportunity to lead presented itself.[4] While there is some validity to the notion that humans (men and women, of course, although Carlyle's examples were all men) are physiologically inclined to lean into unique personality traits and intellectual capacities, the Great Man Theory has largely been debunked by subsequent sociological and behavioral research.

Next came Gordon Allport. The early twentieth century

Harvard psychologist is perhaps best known for his work on human development and the identification of phenotypes and genotypes. His earlier work, however, focused on traits. Allport's Trait Theory aimed to categorize personality traits: (1) cardinal traits—motivators and passions; (2) central traits—qualities all humans possess in varying levels, such as empathy or honesty; and (3) secondary traits—qualities we call personality quirks, which are unique to us as individuals. The Trait Theory of Leadership set out to find common traits of leaders, such as charisma, courage, intelligence, and communication skills.[5] While a trait theory of leaders hasn't been scientifically validated, it became the jumping-off point for behavioral-based studies when it became clear that characteristics of leadership were expressed through behavior and not natural attributes.

Kurt Lewin is one of the founders of modern sociology. In addition to presenting one of the first models of group social mobility, his theories on organizational change have been applied to business and management. In a 1938 paper, Lewin defined three Leadership Climates that can be present in any organization: Authoritarian, Democratic, and Laissez-faire.[6] In an Authoritarian climate, the leader determines and monitors both policy and process; praise and criticism are tied to personal performance. In a modern setting, we would call this extreme micromanagement. In a Democratic climate, decisions are made collectively, with help from the leader; praise is based upon meeting objectives, performance is frequently monitored, and adjustments are made if performance begins to wane. Lastly, in a Laissez-faire climate, the workers make decisions and the leader intervenes only when asked or when necessary, such as in crisis situations; praise and criticism are infrequent and may only occur when an issue arises or at an annual performance review. Later behavioral theories such as Situational Leadership and the Leadership Continuum drew inspiration from Lewin's three social climates.

Early Theories

Carlyle, 1841

Great Man Theory

"The history of the world is but the biography of great men."

Allport, 1937

Trait Theory

Cardinal- passions
Central- all people
Secondary- quirks

Lewin, 1938

Leadership Climates

Authoritarian- dictated
Democratic- collective
Laissez Faire- delegated

You Have to Start Somewhere

Lucy was born in 1964. She was a curious child but rarely left her parents' side. Lucy achieved developmental milestones at an astonishing pace: she held her own bottle at two months, walked by six months, and was eating with a fork and spoon by her first birthday. Despite these achievements, Lucy couldn't speak. However, this setback didn't deter Lucy from communicating with her parents and their friends. She became quite adept at sign language and even made up words for things she hadn't learned yet, like "candy drink" for watermelon and "cry hurt food" when she encountered a rotten radish. These achievements are that much more remarkable when you learn that Lucy was a chimpanzee.

Lucy was taken from her mother on the day she was born and was raised by psychologist Maurice Temerlin and his wife

Jane in their home and at the Institute for Primate Studies at the University of Oklahoma. Temerlin wanted to determine if a chimp who had never interacted with other chimps and was raised like a child would be more like a human child or a primate. Lucy took on many human qualities like making tea for visitors, flipping through magazines, and even blaming her mistakes on researchers at the institute. When introduced to a male chimp, the first nonhuman she had encountered since birth, Lucy was afraid of the animal that most certainly wasn't her kind.[7]

Psychology was a young but growing scientific discipline when Lucy was born. Wilhelm Wundt, the father of modern psychology, had opened the first formal lab less than one hundred years earlier and, like in the early years of leadership theory, many of the earliest theories were based more on conjecture than science. Behaviorism burst onto the scene in the early twentieth century and revolutionized the young discipline. Behaviorists believed that people are born a blank slate (or tabula rasa) and are shaped by their experiences. Early theorist John Watson famously proclaimed in 1913, "Give me a dozen healthy infants, well-formed, and my own specified world to bring them up in and I'll guarantee to take any one at random and train him to become any type of specialist I might select—doctor, lawyer, artist—regardless of his talents, penchants, tendencies, abilities, vocations and race of his ancestors."[8] Famous experiments such as Pavlov's dogs, the Skinner Box, and Little Albert furthered the notoriety and also the notorious nature of the behaviorists. In 1964, Temerlin and Lucy were the latest and perhaps the most provocative of the behaviorist experiments.[9]

As Lucy grew into adolescence, a few problems developed. She grew large and strong. It is estimated that, despite their smaller size, full-grown chimpanzees are two and a half to five times stronger than a person. Despite the Temerlins' interventions, the onset of adolescence swung the needle from human-like behavior to chimpanzee behavior. Lucy would destroy the family home and jump on visitors. She displayed hormonal responses that would be perfectly normal in her natural habitat but were troubling in a human home. The Temerlins loved Lucy beyond the behavioral experiment but knew she could no longer stay with them.

Lucy was moved to a nature preserve on an island off the coast of Gambia, where she could be with other chimps in need of rehabilitation, and placed under the supervision of graduate student Janis Carter. Although Carter intended to ease Lucy's transition to the preserve over a period of weeks, she stayed for years as Lucy struggled to leave her human ways behind. It took time, but eventually the other chimps bonded and Janis was no longer of use to them. But not Lucy. She relied on Janis for food and would often sign "come" followed by "hurt" when Janis wouldn't come to her. One day, Lucy and Janis had a breakthrough. After a particularly hard day, they both laid down to rest. When Janis awoke, Lucy offered her a leaf to eat which Janis returned to Lucy. Perhaps at that moment Lucy realized she was something different from Janis, as she began to forage for her own food thus allowing Janis to leave the island knowing Lucy would be okay.

A commonality shared by early leadership theories and early behaviorist theories is that both sought to address the shortcomings of the previous methods. Great Man Theory, like many early psychology theories, was based on little more than narrow observation. Behaviorism attempted to systematize psychology from a scientific perspective in the same way that Allport and Lewin tried to make sense of leadership. These theories seem arcane and even a bit cruel by modern standards; however, the errors in these early theories became the basis for more sophisticated and scientific research in both psychology and leadership studies. Behavioral psychology gave way to cognitive psychology; trait theories gave way to leadership's own behavioral, cognitive, and emotional studies.

A year after leaving the island, Janis returned to check on Lucy and the other chimpanzees. Hearing her boat, the chimps came out of the brush to see what made the strange sound. Lucy remembered Janis and Janis had brought a few of Lucy's toys, including her favorite mirror. Lucy played with her mirror for a few minutes and then leaned in and gave Janis a hug that was thankfully caught on film as it is a stirring and emotional image. Lucy then joined the rest of her troop (or *shrewdness* if you prefer; both are acceptable names for a group of chimpanzees) and made her way into the jungle without looking back. Lucy had finally become what Janis had always hoped she would be, a chimpanzee—no longer a science experiment.

Chapter 2

Leadership Continuum: Tannenbaum and Schmidt

"There is no accident, just as there is no beginning and no end."

—Jackson Pollock

Many researchers consider the Leadership Continuum to be the first formal leadership theory. It was published in a 1958 edition of the *Harvard Business Review* by Robert Tannenbaum and Warren Schmidt in the article "How to Choose a Leadership Pattern." Although prior ideas existed on organizational leadership, like those of Allport and Lewin, Tannenbaum and Schmidt's work was one of the first academic papers presenting a systematic approach to leadership practice.

Tannenbaum and Schmidt proposed a seven-step continuum that defines leader involvement from "using authority" to "giving freedom." Each step outlines the behavior of the leader along the continuum.

Tells: The leader makes a decision and tells the team what to do.

> *Sells*: The leader makes the decision and sells it to the team.
> *Suggests*: The leader suggests a course of action and invites questions from the team.
> *Consults*: The leader consults the team before making the final decision.
> *Joins*: The leader presents the problem, gets the team's input, and then makes the decision.
> *Delegates*: The leader defines boundaries and then asks the team to make the decision.
> *Abdicates*: The leader allows the team to make the decision.[10]

While these seven steps are pretty straightforward, the second part of Tannenbaum and Schmidt's theory outlines the forces that influence decision-making. Finding the right balance of forces helps the leader determine where on the continuum the decision should fall. Forces at work in the leader include their values, confidence in personal decision-making, and confidence in the team's ability to make decisions. Forces at work in the team include their style and dynamic, how confident they are in each other, and how much they trust the leader. Lastly, the forces of the situation are dictated by how important the decision is, if a wrong move may create a cascade, the priority of the project, and the track record of both the leader and the team.

The gradual release of responsibility in the Leadership Continuum is similar to the "show me, help me, let me" educational model proposed by David Pearson and Margaret Gallagher in the 1980s.[11] Pearson and Gallagher's model became the preferred way to teach children to read and is the basis for "instructional scaffolding" whereby teachers build students' understanding one piece at a time until instruction on the concept is no longer necessary.

Gradual release of responsibility dates back even further than Tannenbaum and Schmidt. Early twentieth century Russian psychologist Lev Vygotsky suggested that planned obsolescence should be the purpose of teaching. Vygotsky's Zone of Proximal Development defined all skills as fitting into one of three zones: (Z1) things we can do, (Z2) things we can do with assistance, and (Z3) things we cannot do even with assistance.[12] For example, I can balance my checkbook (Z1). I can file my taxes with the assistance of my accountant (Z2). I can't do theoretical physics (Z3). If my accountant were to teach me how to file my taxes, perhaps that task could move from Zone 2 to Zone 1. I am fairly confident, however, that particle physics will always remain in my Zone 3.

Leadership Continuum
Tannenbaum and Schmidt

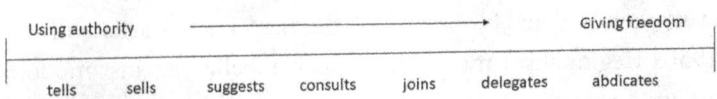

"I Taught Jack That"

Laverne and Shirley. Felix and Oscar. Riggs and Murtaugh. Film and TV have shown us time and time again that odd pairings can create great things. Real life also occasionally offers up what appears to be a strange mentor–mentee relationship that produces exceptional results.

The artist Jackson Pollock lived a vagabond lifestyle as a young man bouncing around the American West. He was born in Wyoming and taken to California by his mother as a baby. He grew up in Arizona and a few different locations in California, his unsettled nature evident in his expulsion from two high schools before his seventeenth birthday. In 1930, he and his brother Charles settled in New York City and took up residence at the Art Students League, which was then and continues today as an informal art school that confers no degrees. Although Pollock is their most famous "alum," maritime artist Winslow Homer and crooner Tony Bennett spent time there as well. The instructor who took a liking to the young Pollock was muralist Thomas Hart Benton. Even if you don't recognize Benton's name, his Depression Era, WPA-funded projects figure prominently in just about every history textbook you can find.

Benton and Pollock could not have had more disparate upbringings. Benton was the son of a Missouri congressman. He split his time between Kansas City and Washington D.C. and was afforded every opportunity befitting a lawmaker's son, including studying in New York and Paris after serving in World War I. But that's not to say Benton didn't possess exceptional talent. He is one of the best-known artists of the 1930s Regionalism movement, which rebelled against modern art and focused on Americana and the portrayal of marginalized groups.[13] Famous works like *The Cotton Pickers* and *Persephone* are housed at the Art Institute of Chicago and Nelson-Atkins Museum of Art in Kansas City.

Benton is considered to be Pollock's only art teacher. They studied together for five years, traveling the West where Benton taught Pollock form and figure drawing, which would play a prominent role in Pollock's famous drip paintings. Although it would seem Benton's murals and Pollock's drips are as different as their childhoods, this formative training in the ways of art became the foundation of everything Pollock would paint. Benton was not only a mentor but became a surrogate father and personal hero to Pollock. The esteem was mutual as Benton included Pollock as a model in a number of his most prominent works including the ten-panel *America Today* mural, which has its own room at the Metropolitan Museum of Art.

Benton permanently moved to his native Missouri in 1935 where he continued mural work and taught at the Kansas City Art Institute. Pollock remained in New York, thus ending their professional relationship. After Benton's departure, Pollock's career skyrocketed as he won world renown for "drip period" pieces like *Number 11 (Blue Poles)* and *Number 17A* which posthumously sold for $200 million in 2015. Although they never formally worked together again, Benton and Pollock remained close until Pollock's untimely death at the height of his popularity in 1956.

Benton displayed remarkable mentorship and leadership in helping Pollock develop. His lessons followed the gradual "release of responsibility" model in a way that helped Pollock develop technically and still find his vision. The landscapes and portraits of frontier life that Pollock drew with Benton evolved into abstract sketches that eventually became Pollock's famous drip paintings. When Pollock blossomed into the artist he hoped to be, Benton's lessons were still present, albeit hidden. There are figures within those paint drips, and the dark, steely blues are purposefully similar to the dark background used by Benton.

Benton followed the "tells," "sells," and "suggests" stages, allowing Pollock to incorporate the lessons into his own evolving vision of art, until his teacher moved on to "delegating" and "abdicating." Both artists were considered innovators at the height of their fame but in different ways: Benton rejected modernity and focused on traditional subjects; Pollock rejected modernity in favor of abstract interpretations. Had Benton not mentored Pollock in the way he did, perhaps "Jack the Dripper" would have been another generation of folk artist instead of the most successful abstract artist since Picasso.

Mentorship is how new professionals find their way and how leaders transfer the profession's legacy to the next generation. In the Leadership Continuum, the leader is heavily involved at the low levels; the outcomes at the higher levels belong to the pupil and may go in an entirely different but wildly successful direction, as was the case with Pollock. Despite different products and the evolving views of any profession, a good mentor–mentee relationship achieves the same goals. Benton and Pollock both sought to portray the volatility of America at the time in which they were working. Benton painted cotton pickers and industrial workers. Pollock's abstract expressionism asked the viewer to find a sense of organization in the perceived chaos. Yet both achieved their goal.

Vygotsky theorized that all teaching and mentoring is planned obsolescence, as none of us will work, or for that matter live, forever. When it is time to pass the torch, leaders do not get to choose the methods of the next generation but they hopefully have prepared them for the challenges ahead.

Chapter 3

Bases of Power: French and Raven

"A crown is merely a hat that lets the rain in."
—Frederick the Great

Psychologists John French and Bertram Raven introduced their theory of Bases of Power as a chapter in the 1959 book *Studies in Social Power, edited by Dorwin Cartwright*. The team identified five different forms of power: Legitimate, Reward, Coercive, Referent, and Expert. Raven expanded the list in 1965 to include Informational as the sixth power base.[14]

To understand each base, we first have to establish a definition of power. French and Raven viewed power as related to social influence and persuasion; that is, the ability to say or do something that influences a person to comply with a request or change their behavior. Each base is an example of a type of power that leaders can leverage.

Legitimate power is established through an agreed-upon position or status. Leaders gain legitimacy through being hired, elected, or appointed to a position. Employees legitimize the leader's power by accepting that person as a supervisor. Organizational charts and job descriptions outline roles and therefore establish the power tied to each position. In the legitimate power model, the employee accepts the boss's prerogative to ask them to change a behavior to better achieve the goals of the organization. The employee doesn't necessarily have to agree with the change but accepts the legitimacy of the request.

Reward power is established through the leader's positive motivation of their employees. A few common examples are monetary bonuses, additional time off, formalized praise, or providing mentoring; that is, all things the employee wants. Rewards can also be the removal of something the employee doesn't want; for instance, new employees often go through a probationary period, typically ninety days. The removal of that probationary label is a reward for proving to be a good fit for the organization. The leader needs to be mindful when working within a reward structure, as a leader may become ineffective when they overpromise and cannot deliver. Reward power is popular because it creates a win-win situation if done correctly. The employee is happy with the reward and the leader is viewed favorably for making it happen.

Coercive power is the opposite of reward power in that the supervisor gives the employee something they don't want; that is, punishment or the potential for punishment. A few examples are a teacher assigning a bad grade for poor performance, a boss giving a written reprimand to an employee for inappropriate behavior, or a low-performing employee being assigned to a less desirable project. It is interesting to note that French and Raven discovered that, while the severity of the punishment was influential, it was the certainty of punishment that had the greatest effect on the employee. For example, you may drive a little too quickly from time to time. While the punishments for speeding can be quite daunting, the certainty of getting caught is relatively minimal. Now imagine if the police devised a system in which every speeding driver got caught every time. The certainty of being caught would serve as a greater deterrent than the size of the punishment.

Referent power draws from a leader's charisma and the desire of the follower to emulate the leader. In this case, I use the word "follower" instead of "employee," as referent power often refers to an inspirational person who isn't a supervisor at work. Our heroes possess referent power and we generally don't know them personally. Children of the 1980s like myself probably remember the Gatorade commercial that told us we could "Be like Mike." The ad showed a bunch of kids practicing basketball with Michael Jordan (while a very catchy jingle played) and reaching for a Gatorade when they needed a refreshing break. Michael Jordan wasn't our boss but he was cool, which made us all want to be like Mike even if we were no good at basketball. Followers of referent leaders gain a sense of oneness and belonging to a group identity. A more contemporary example is Taylor Swift's posse of "Swifties." Their devotion to Taylor and her music is unrivaled and not only aspires to the greatness of their favorite artist but also creates a sense of community, identity, and satisfaction that the group can share.

Expert power is derived from knowledge and expertise in any field whether it be medicine or macrame. Followers (again, they may not be employees) acknowledge and accept that the expert has insight and experience they do not. Because the follower trusts the expert, they don't feel the need to understand the detailed aspects of the task. If a scan shows that

I have an inflamed appendix, I wouldn't feel the need to learn how to safely remove the offending organ because I trust the surgeon who has been trained and routinely removes people's appendixes. Expert power is also unique to the individual. If I lose trust in my lawyer and fire him, he ceases to be my lawyer but he doesn't cease to be a lawyer. His expert status may have ended in my mind but he is still an expert who has the trust of his other clients.

Bases of Power

French and Raven

Legitimate	position, status
Reward	things you want/ removal of things you don't
Coercive	ability to punish or potential to punish
Referent	charisma, inspiration
Expert	knowledge, expertise
Informational	use of persuasive reasoning

The last base is Informational power. This concept is more abstract than the first five bases, as informational power is a commodity that can be shared. Insight into a process or results of a research study are pieces of information that present persuasive reasons why a task should be done differently. Informational power is exercised upon an individual when they are introduced to new knowledge, consider its value, and then ultimately decide to make a change based on the worth of the knowledge. This is different from Expert power because it is the knowledge that moves the follower to act, not the reputation of the person presenting it. For example, if I want to lose weight, I may watch a video or attend a lecture on healthy diet and exercise. Assuming the presenter isn't a famous fitness guru, I am not influenced by them as much as I am influenced by the information that has been presented. I have bought into the informational power of the message once I have evaluated the information and decided that it will help me achieve my goal; the process occurs independent of my feelings about the speaker.

The Tortoise and the Hare
To delve more deeply into French and Raven's Bases of Power, let's consider two identical universes where the only difference is who is in charge of a sales team. Everything other than the leader is the same, including the company's budget, the employees that work for him/her/them, and the market within which the sales will occur. The leader's actions are the only factor affecting the outcome.

(1) Alex was recently promoted to Director of Sales, and they have three regional salespeople (which Alex was allowed to choose) who report to them. The company is structured so that several sales teams compete with one another. The best-performing teams receive the best rewards. Alex grew up in the area, attended the local university, and has been with the company for over ten years. They are charismatic and were promoted, in large part, because people respond to their kind and friendly nature. Alex's highest value asset is their knack for naturally inspiring those around them to want to be the best. At the first team meeting, Alex told the team,

"We're going to figure out the best path forward together. I'll supply the resources; you all deliver on our shared vision." After working together for a few months, the team has come together as hoped and their sales numbers have been consistently growing. Alex recently attended a conference where a market analyst presented a theory that could be useful to the company, after which Alex met with the team, explained the idea, and why they think the team should implement it. The team agreed to give it a try.

(2) Taylor was recently promoted to Director of Sales, and they have three regional salespeople (which Taylor was allowed to choose) who report to them. The company is structured so that several sales teams compete with one another. Taylor graduated from a top MBA program and has been with the company for four years. Taylor's sales numbers are fantastic, which led to the promotion. Taylor has been described as intense but also as the kind of person whose success rubs off on others. At the first team meeting, Taylor told the team, "You're on this team because I handpicked the best salespeople we have. I expect you to perform because I already know what you are capable of. It is imperative that you commit and keep up." After working together for a few months, the team has come together and is working well. Their sales numbers started out very strong and have remained relatively consistent. Taylor recently attended a conference where

a market analyst presented a theory that could be useful to the company, after which Taylor met with the team and said they have been doing well but need to implement this new idea to put them "over the top." The team nodded with approval.

Which leader is doing a better job? Which leader will be more successful in the long term? Which leader would you want to work for? Taylor's approach is aggressive, which may rub some people the wrong way, but that team has been pulling in the bigger bonuses from the start. Alex's team is more harmonious and has been making improvements but isn't finishing near the top. The push and pull you feel when reading about these two leadership styles is a direct result of the struggle for power. A team like Taylor's is focused on performance that leads to maximum reward and is therefore quite demanding. A team like Alex's is focused on steady, incremental growth. The reward isn't as great but neither is the pressure to perform.

While the *Tortoise and the Hare* taught us that the "slow and steady" tortoise wins the race because the overconfident hare eventually tires and falters at the end, French and Raven present both sides of the story. The referent leader (Alex) steadily improves the team and provides them with a stable pace toward the finish line with a combination of consistent reward and minimal threat of coercion. The expert leader (Taylor), heavy on reward but also heavy on coercion, pushes the team to the finish line and maximum reward, with the understanding that poor performance means you're going to be left in the ditch. Being on Alex's team may make you feel good but it provides a foggier vision of success. Taylor's team may be pressure-packed but they are certainly focused on success. This hard decision exists in any competitive environment, which is exactly what makes French and Raven's Bases of Power timeless and perpetually relevant.

Chapter 4

The ~~M~~ichigan and Ohio State Leadership Studies

"It just means more at Ohio State."
—Justin Fields, former Buckeyes quarterback (probably not talking about the Michigan and Ohio State Leadership Studies)

There is nothing wrong with your vision: the "M" in "Michigan" is indeed crossed out in this chapter's title above. You see, Ohio State vs. University of Michigan is one of the most heated rivalries in college football; you'll learn just how the strikethrough "M" factors into that rivalry as you read on. However, when it comes to leadership studies, the two colleges have functioned in a remarkably symbiotic way. The well-known and often cited University of Michigan Leadership Studies and the Ohio State University Leadership Studies possess a lot of similarities, and they have been combined historically to give a comprehensive picture of progressive leadership theory published in post–World War II America.

While many people worked on the series of studies at

Michigan, one of the more recognizable names was Rensis Likert (yes, the inventor of the Likert scale—the "Strongly Disagree" to "Strongly Agree" bubbles we all love to fill out on surveys). The Michigan studies aimed to identify characteristics of organizations that contribute to high productivity and high job satisfaction. The team came up with two categories: job-oriented leadership and employee-oriented leadership.[15] In job-oriented leadership, the main areas of focus are increased production and limiting mistakes. In employee-oriented leadership, the primary focus is on establishing relationships with employees that will build trust.

Leaders who implemented the job-oriented style reported spending more time managing employee performance to identify strong and weak individuals or teams. Employee-oriented leaders spent more time on decision-making and goal-focused work. Not surprisingly, employees preferred employee-oriented leadership; however, they reported it was preferred in large part because they didn't fear making mistakes or reporting errors. While job-oriented leadership's purpose is to limit mistakes, it may inadvertently create a culture where employees fear reporting inevitable mistakes. This is especially dangerous as hidden problems could linger and not be addressed due to a lack of awareness. The Michigan studies continued throughout the 1950s and ultimately concluded that the best approach was to be employee-focused first but also to emphasize production.

The Ohio State University Leadership Studies took place in the same era as their counterparts at Michigan. Frequently cited researchers from the Ohio State studies are Ralph Stogdill and Andrew Halpin. The OSU study developed the Leader Behavior Description Questionnaire (LBDQ) and surveyed military leaders[16]. The LBDQ measures comfort with actions such as setting standards, soliciting input, clarifying roles, and creating plans of action. Interestingly, modern versions of the LBDQ use Likert scales. The results of the surveys found that leaders fit into two categories: consideration-focused and structure-focused.[17]

Similar to employee-oriented, leaders who scored high in the consideration category were found to value interpersonal skills that expressed appreciation for colleagues and maintained an amiable work environment. Leaders who scored high in initiating structure were similar to the job-oriented leaders from the University of Michigan study. These leaders focused on increasing production by assigning tasks and monitoring objective measures.

The findings of the OSU study were so similar to the Michigan study that their conclusion was to formalize the interaction between their two categories by plotting scores on an x and y axis to create four quadrants: (I) Low Consideration & Low Initiating Structure, (II) Low Consideration & High Initiating Structure, (III) High Consideration & Low Initiating Structure, and (IV) High Consideration & High Initiating Structure. The Michigan study only identified their two categories as high or low. While Ohio State's system was more formalized, the work of the two universities combined nicely into one model.

Michigan and Ohio State Leadership Studies

Job-oriented or Employee-oriented

III. High consideration/ Low initiating	IV. High consideration/ High initiating
I. Low consideration/ Low initiating	II. Low consideration/ High initiating

Consideration (left axis)

Initiating (bottom axis)

Crossing Out the M's

The football teams of Ohio State and University of Michigan first met in 1897, and have played every season from 1918 to 2020—from the end of WWI until COVID-19. Both teams play in the Big Ten and their campuses in Columbus, Ohio, and Ann Arbor, Michigan, are less than two hundred miles apart. Ohio State has come up with a novel way to show its disdain for its biggest rival: namely, crossing out all the M's that can be found around Columbus during the week of the game. Academic buildings, street signs, restaurants, and even people's mailboxes are not spared a red X covering every M in a word.

ESPN summarized the Ohio State–Michigan rivalry pretty well in two commercials. In one, a young couple kiss while professing their love for one another. The man is wearing an Ohio State shirt and the woman is wearing a Michigan shirt. The caption that appears on the screen says, "Without sports, this wouldn't be disgusting." In another, an older man and woman are on a blind date driving to dinner. They chat about their jobs and where they are from until the woman exclaims, "Michigan, born and raised. Go Blue!" (The University of Michigan's colors are maize and blue.) The man's face sours and he jumps from the moving vehicle. After rolling down a hill, he stands and yells, "Go Buckeyes!" (which is the nickname of 'thee' Ohio State University).

The games have often been as strange as the rivalry itself.[18] The Snow Bowl, as it became known, was played in 1950 during one of the biggest snowstorms in Ohio history. Visibility was so bad that both teams decided to punt the ball when they didn't have to in hopes that their opponents would fumble it in the end zone. Michigan won that game 9-3, which begs the question: how did the teams combine to kick four field goals in a blizzard? In 1968, OSU beat Michigan 50-14, yet they attempted a 2-point conversion after their last touchdown. When asked why he went for two when the game was already a blowout, famed Ohio State coach Woody Hayes answered, "Because they wouldn't let me go for three."[19]

Speaking of Hayes, the most competitive years of the rivalry came between 1969 and 1978 when Hayes squared off against his former protégé, the highly successful Michigan head coach Bo Schembechler. These meetings were dubbed the Ten Year War. In 1973, both teams entered the game undefeated and played to a tie. Thanks to that tie, Schembechler emerged victorious in the Ten Year War (Michigan won 5-4-1) with the series ending in 1978 after Hayes was forced into retirement for punching an opposing player.

Fast forward to the 2006 Game of the Century. The teams were set to meet yet again with undefeated records. In a tragic twist, Bo Schembechler died the night before the game. Remember, Coach Schembechler had ties to both universities. A video tribute to Schembechler was about the only thing the crowd agreed to clap for that night in Columbus. The #1 Buckeyes edged out the #2 ranked Wolverines by a score of 42-39. What were the Ohio Pick 4 lottery results that night? Of course, the winning numbers mimicked the final score, 4-2-3-9.

To date, Michigan has won eleven national titles to Ohio State's seven. However, Ohio State boasts seven Heisman Trophy winners to Michigan's three. I'll let you decide which is more important. As a Notre Dame fan, I shouldn't care for either one, but there is one last important Woody Hayes anecdote to share. Hayes claimed to be Notre Dame's best recruiter: He would steer any recruit that he couldn't convince to come to Ohio State to consider Notre Dame—something about Catholic virtues and strong academics did the trick with most parents. Woody was no dummy. Ohio State didn't play Notre Dame but Michigan did, so you might as well have the guys you can't get to play for you beat up on your biggest rival.

You may be thinking, what does this story have to do with the Michigan and Ohio State leadership studies? It may be a tenuous connection, but it highlights the importance of working together. From the storytelling standpoint, it is curious how two heated rival colleges came together to create one of the most influential leadership models of the twentieth century. The Michigan and Ohio State studies changed the way American industry leaders thought about business throughout the Cold War Era, characterized by competition with the Russians. So come on, let's get it together! We can put aside football differences and use the Research 1 institution resources at our disposal to do something great again. Go Irish!

Chapter 5

Theories X and Y: McGregor

"I once worked with a guy for three years and never learned his name. Best friend I ever had. We still never talk sometimes."

—*Parks & Recreation*'s
Ron Swanson on management

Some leadership theories are formed based on perceptions of the average worker's inherent motivation to contribute in a meaningful way as an employee and a member of society. Two such theories were created by social psychologist Douglas McGregor, who worked with Kurt Lewin at the famed Sloan School of Management on the campus of the Massachusetts Institute of Technology when it opened in 1952. McGregor applied Lewin's ideas on social climate to leadership through what he called Theory X and Theory Y in his 1960 book, *The Human Side of Enterprise*. He also worked with psychologist Abraham Maslow to align Theory X and Theory Y with Maslow's Hierarchy of Needs.[20] McGregor's Theory X assumes employees don't want to work and have little ambition. Therefore, they would show little initiative if left to their own devices. This is similar to Lewin's

Authoritarian climate in that it calls for management to take a hands-on approach where all outcomes can be traced back to the employee who completed the task; it also corresponds to the lower levels of Maslow (i.e., basic needs and safety). In contrast, Theory Y focuses on employee autonomy with guidance from management since employees want to work and are self-motivated. Employees complete tasks independently but leadership ensures their efforts work toward meeting the company's goals.[21] This is similar to Lewin's Democratic climate and aligns with the middle levels of Maslow's pyramid (i.e., belonging and esteem).

Theory Z: Ouchi

So, we have Theory X equating to an Authoritarian climate and low-level Maslow, and Theory Y equating to a Democratic climate and mid-level Maslow. There has to be a Theory Z equating to a Laissez-faire climate and the top of Maslow's pyramid, right? A few researchers proposed a Theory Z, including Maslow himself. If you are familiar with the Hierarchy of Needs, you likely picture self-actualization at the top, as that is generally accepted as the highest goal. Once an individual has established psychological needs, safety, belonging, love, and self-esteem, all that seems to be left is to become their best self. In Maslow's version of Theory Z, however, someone who has reached self-actualization transcends their own life by living free of want and crafting a legacy larger than themselves. Having studied individuals who had reached self-actualization yet strived for something more, Maslow believed it was necessary to add a transcendence stage to his hierarchy.

Nevertheless, the researcher who is credited with drawing a direct line from Y to Z, and also including Lewin's Laissez-faire climate, is William Ouchi in his 1981 book, *Theory Z: How American Business Can Meet the Japanese Challenge*. While I recognize I just jumped straight to 1981, this work corresponds with McGregor. We'll return to the 1960s with the next theory. Although born and educated in America, Ouchi has strong ties to his Japanese heritage and a strong interest in how Japanese industry had burst into the electronics and automobile markets during the 1970s. Ouchi's Theory Z contends that the promise of stable long-term employment and permission for employees to focus their efforts on projects that meet their expertise and interests leads to the creation of innovative products.[22] This notion draws a clearer comparison to Lewin's Laissez-faire climate, in which employees are encouraged to pursue their solutions with advisement from management when necessary, while also illustrating Maslow's vision of self-actualization.

Theories X and Y- McGregor | Theory Z- Ouchi

Theory	Climate	Hierarchy of Need
Theory X	Authoritarian	Low Maslow
Theory Y	Democratic	Medium Maslow
Theory Z	Laissez-Faire	High Maslow

Regular Hours?

The notion of working in an Authoritarian climate may bring to mind a prison camp but many industrial jobs follow this structure. Any job with an agreed upon "clock in" and "clock out" time follows McGregor's Theory X. Employees agree to trade their time and effort for compensation. Factory jobs, food service, hospitality, and retail are all examples of this climate, and those jobs make up huge swaths of the economy. The work may not be thrilling but the employee enjoys knowing that their time off the clock is entirely their own. Any overtime outside the agreed-upon shift tends to come with a pretty nice bump in the hourly rate. This model of "punching the clock" isn't perfect, as it relies on objective verification as opposed to fundamental trust. It can interfere with building personal relationships and a sense of goodwill or solidarity between employees and managers.

Professional jobs may follow a variation of this pattern. When I was a teacher, my school day was made up of eight 43-minute periods. Everyone had a 30-minute lunch and every teacher had one free period for prep. The day was very regimented. Teachers arrived by 7:35 each morning. The doors opened to students at 7:50. Students were released to the halls and their lockers at 8:00. First period started at 8:12. (Keep in mind, I have not been in this job for roughly six years yet I still remember the times to the minute!) My prep period was around 9:00 and lunch was around noon. Any other needs (e.g., bathroom, phone call, copier) had to occur in 3-minute bursts between classes.

While the principal of our school was not an authoritarian leader, and the actual preparation, teaching, and assessment of students followed a Theory Y/Democratic model, the schedule of a high school requires a relatively controlled environment focused on Maslow's basic needs of safety and belonging to the school community for the sake of students' learning and stability. Since that schedule also needs to be implemented and followed by teachers, staff, and administrators, it made for an interesting hybrid of Theories X and Y.

In 2023, both the *New York Times* and the *San Francisco Chronicle*[23] declared the Five-Day Office Week dead. Journalists at the *Times* reported a 50 percent decline in in-office work attendance since February 2020.[24] The numbers were even higher in the Bay Area. When people were forced to work from home because of the COVID-19 pandemic, many found the improved work–life balance attractive and sought to keep that lifestyle once it was safe to return to the office. Employees were choosier about where they would work based on the flexibility employers could offer. Employers were able to reap benefits from this arrangement as well: costly leases on office space could be allowed to expire if employees no longer needed the physical office to get their work done.

The work-from-home boom provides an intriguing example of Theory Y at play. It's not the controlled environment of Theory X, yet not the freedom of Theory Z; it is as true a middle mark as you can find. Employees are trusted to get their work done to the standards of the company they work for. Managers ensure that work is completed to a quality standard, consolidate projects, and report results to leadership. This model also allows leadership to recruit talent more broadly. After all, if your employees don't necessarily have to be in the building then why do they need to be in the same city, state, or even country?

Theory Z is often associated with liberal leave time, a luxury that many college professors enjoy. The expectation for most professors is to teach, conduct scholarship, and perform service through acts such as serving on academic committees, advising students, or working in the community. Teaching is the only part that needs to occur at a specific time, so most other job duties are left to the professor's discretion. In essence, the expectation of being an expert in your field means that you have committed yourself to what it is that you study. For this reason, it would be counterproductive to tell a chemist to only research new drugs from 9:00 a.m. to 4:00 p.m. or a psychologist working on a book to only write from 8:30 a.m. to 4:30 p.m., with a half-hour lunch, of course. Once scholarship became a part of my job, I realized how true the notion of "professor hours" really is. I might work from 8:00 a.m. to 4:00 p.m. one day, 10:00 a.m. to 10:00 p.m. the next, a couple of hours on a Saturday, or any other combination. Most of what you are reading was done in the evenings, as I try to devote my time during the day to students.

The laissez-faire nature of Theory Z is not just for professors though. Gig workers, tax preparers, gardeners, artists, and any independent contractor with the ability to work when they want to are practicing Theory Z. While this may sound heavenly, the lack of structure means you have to keep yourself on track. Taxes have due dates and clients have other options. The business of art can be especially brutal and burdens some of society's most talented people with a perpetual need to produce in order to remain relevant. Maslow's view of Theory Z applies to these lifestyles as workers have the flexibility in time and application of talent to work toward the best versions of their professional selves. Professors are free to pursue the research they feel is most valuable. Artists can paint, sculpt, and write the works that are most meaningful to them. Lawyers are free to pursue the cases they think are most important to freedom and justice. It's a laissez-faire life but somebody's got to live it.

From a leadership standpoint, implementing the correct climate or theory depends on the industry, the company's goals, and the makeup of the team. If the goal is innovation, employees need space to innovate through planning, testing, and experimenting. If the goal is output, employees need time and materials to manufacture whatever it is the company produces. Nevertheless, it certainly doesn't hurt to build in flexibility wherever possible. Those rare last days of the school term when the students went home early and the principal got on the overhead speaker to tell the teachers they could leave as well were priceless.

Chapter 6

Contingency Model: Fiedler

> "We should never want to become anyone else because the greatest fulfillment we can ever get out of life is by becoming the best possible version of ourselves."
>
> —Alexi Pappas

In 1964, Fred Fiedler proposed "A Contingency Model of Leadership Effectiveness." According to the Contingency Model, there is no "best" leadership style; rather Fiedler suggests the leader should focus on implementing the best action given the situation. An individual adapts to the circumstances and responds with the best course of action even when that action may not produce the optimal outcome. To determine the correct action, the leader must consider both their leadership style and the favorableness of the situation.[25]

Fiedler believed that leadership style is fixed and based on personality. While it is possible to make changes to be more extroverted or learn better communication skills, most people default back to what feels natural to them. To measure leadership capacity, he created the somewhat comically named Least Preferred Coworker (LPC) scale, an eighteen-question Likert scale from one to eight that measures characteristics on a continuum such as Supportive/Hostile, Open/Guarded, and Harmonious/Quarrelsome. The scale isn't very specific, but it doesn't have to be, since the final score is meant to simply inform a leader's practice. After plotting their perceived score for each item, the leader adds up their scores and receives either a Low (>57), Mid (57–63), or High (<63) score. Leaders with lower scores tend to be good in straightforward and task-oriented scenarios. Those with high scores tend to be strong in more complex relationship-oriented scenarios. The effectiveness of the LPC scale relies on the leaders being honest with themselves when considering their personalities.

The second element of the Contingency Model is Situational Favorableness. Determining the favorability of a situation is based on three factors: Leader–Member Relationship, Task Structure, and the Leader's Position of Power. The Leader–Member Relationship is reciprocal and speaks to the level of trust and confidence between the leader and their employees. Task Structure concerns the group's knowledge of how to succeed: are the tasks easily understood and is success clearly defined? Finally, the Leader's Position of Power is defined by the leader's ability to make a final decision. Do they have to check with their supervisor or does the buck stop with them?

The key question in Fiedler's Contingency Model is, What does success look like? The leader must be able to read the situation and then decide how to move forward to achieve the best result for their team, keeping in mind that sometimes the best result for the team isn't necessarily the best overall result. This caveat is vital to understanding the Contingency Model and the lesson presented in the story below.

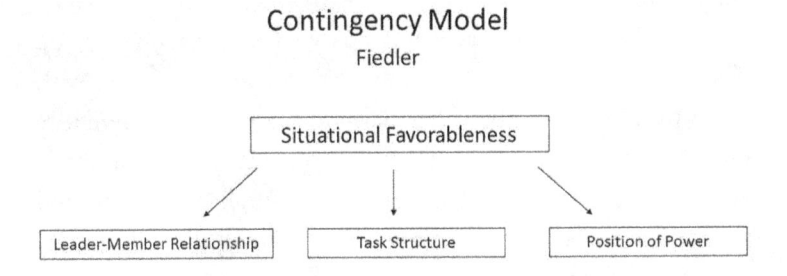

Contingency Model
Fiedler

```
              Situational Favorableness
              /          |          \
Leader-Member Relationship   Task Structure   Position of Power
```

The 10K Runner

Olympians train their whole lives for a chance to represent their country for a few weeks during either the Summer or Winter Olympics. The physical and mental toll on the individual is immense. The athletes' families also commit huge quantities of time, money, and effort to help their loved ones achieve their dreams. I'm not going to pretend I know anything about Olympic training. My track and field career ended just one day into a walk-on effort at my Division II university. Running and jumping were so much harder after a semester of drinking three nights a week (sorry, Mom) and eating pizza whenever I wanted.

In the book *Bravey: Chasing Dreams, Befriending Pain, and Other Big Ideas*, Greek Olympian Alexi Pappas gives her fellow runners the advice to "keep your pace and run your race."[26] At the 2016 Summer Olympics in Rio, Pappas was lapped in the women's 10,000 meters by the eventual winner who set a new world record and finished almost two full minutes ahead of Pappas. Alexi cited one important piece of advice given to her by her coach before the race. She was essentially told, "You're never going to catch this girl so don't even try." Most sports anecdotes say that if you work hard and believe in yourself, you can overcome and achieve, but sometimes hard work and belief simply aren't enough.

The only thing you can control is your performance. If you chase the person who is way out in front, you may hang with them for a while, but you can't sustain that pace for the entire race. You must run your race; don't try to run someone else's. A 10K is a long race. The very best complete it in around thirty minutes with most competitors finishing in around forty minutes. Your career is also long, probably thirty years if your focus is saving for retirement but more than likely closer to forty. You can't "gut" your way through 10,000 meters any easier than you would a thirty to forty year career.

Right now, you might be thinking, *Bummer, why even try?* The simple answer is that your race is beautiful because it belongs to you. Your race isn't any less important than the people who run faster and longer than you. In fact, your race is often the *most* important to the people you care about and who care about you. My kids don't care if I'm a professor at the top-ranked university in the country or one closer to the bottom of those notably flawed rankings. What they will care about (even if they don't understand what it means) is when Dad is promoted to associate professor or maybe someday full professor, because they can then share in the joy of the accomplishment. Those closest to you see the work that you put in every day and want to celebrate your successes with you.

So what does the Contingency Model have to say about Alexi's situation? She finished in seventeenth place in the 10,000 meters at Rio but also set the all-time Greek record. Her best and most realistic outcome was not the overall best outcome. Alexi wasn't going to win gold but her coach knew she could break her home country's record. Alexi also used her celebrity status to become an advocate for mental health and promote a greater understanding of depression in athletes. Athletes, and anyone else who trains for a life-defining goal, are often left with a "what's next" mentality whether they achieve or fail at what they set out to do.

Perhaps you have just been promoted and can't help but start thinking about the next promotion. I get it: as soon as I earned my doctorate, I started focusing on finding a professorship. We get so wrapped up in achieving the goal that we don't plan for the aftermath or prepare for a respite of recovery or celebration. It's important to pause and recognize what needs to be mourned or celebrated before you can move on. Alexi highlighted this notion in *Bravey*. (In case you're wondering, that word comes from her motivational phrase: "Run like a bravey, sleep like a baby, dream like crazy, replace can't with maybe, through sunny and shady.") She came to the conclusion that, while the highlight of her running career may have been the day at the Olympics when she set a national record, it wasn't the highlight of her life's journey or her life's work.

You don't have to win *the* race; strive to win *your* race.

Chapter 7

Stages of Group Development: Tuckman

> "Fly and be free."
> —The phrase a long-forgotten English professor ended our classes with during my freshman year. (Apparently her message stuck with me but not her name.)

Teamwork is an integral part of just about all organizations. A purposeful and focused approach to teaming builds a foundation for effective team functioning and provides employees with opportunities to practice team roles, including leadership skills. Some teams are together for the long haul; others complete projects within a set timeline. Even if a team won't be together long term, leaders should implement strategies to increase efficiency and promote the overall happiness of the team. Team satisfaction is not only important to the goals of the project at hand but also strengthens bonds for future work together.

Developing collaboration and problem-solving skills creates flexibility that can be applied to a broad range of projects. Teams provide a great environment for emerging leaders to practice the skills necessary to one day spearhead their own project and to grow within the organization.

Bruce Tuckman was an educational psychologist who specialized in group dynamics. His Tuckman Model of Team Development was defined in two papers: "Development Sequence in Small Groups"[27] in 1965 and "Stages of Small-Group Development Revisited"[28] in 1977. Tuckman's model states that teams develop and disband in five sequential steps: forming, storming, norming, performing, and adjourning. The Tuckman stages align fairly well with the Leadership Continuum discussed earlier.

Forming: As the name suggests, the team forms during this stage. Everyone is just getting to know each other and is on their best behavior. The mood is generally friendly and courteous (hopefully). During the forming stage, the leader outlines goals and what is expected of the group. This leader's role during the forming stage is similar to the tells and sells stages of the Leadership Continuum.

Storming: The storming stage doesn't only refer to brainstorming, but this is the stage where team members start bouncing ideas off of one another. Once people understand the objectives, it is natural for them to want to solve the problem in their way; however, too many different opinions can cause conflict within the team. At this stage, the leader is acting as a coach by encouraging the team to build consensus, and thus the leader may need to find a compromise to encourage harmony and greater productivity. This role is similar to the suggests and consults stages of the Leadership Continuum.

Norming: At the norming stage, team members have gained a better understanding of each other's expertise and motivations, thereby gaining an appreciation for what each member has to contribute. During the norming stage, the leader acts as a facilitator and asks guiding questions like, "What's the plan?" or "What do you see as potential challenges?" In this case, the leader is practicing the joins stage of the Leadership Continuum.

Performing: The performing stage is where the work gets done. The team knows what they need to do and has a clear vision of how to achieve it. The leader at this stage is delegating responsibility, overseeing the project, and helping the group develop their leaders, practicing the delegates and abdicates stages on the Leadership Continuum.

Adjourning: Finally, the team must adjourn. Nothing lasts forever, all good things must come to an end, nothing gold can stay, please continue inserting other clichés here. As the team disbands, it is important for the leader to reward and recognize the work of the group as well as debrief and summarize the process from start to finish with the team so that everyone leaves with a similar understanding and sense of accomplishment.

Stages of Group Development
Tuckman

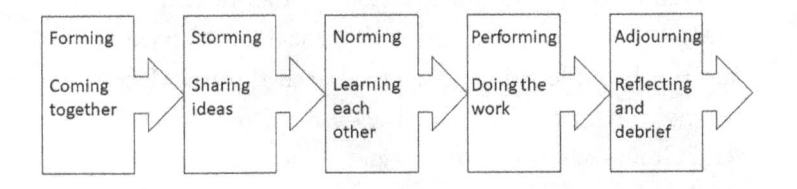

Forming	Storming	Norming	Performing	Adjourning
Coming together	Sharing ideas	Learning each other	Doing the work	Reflecting and debrief

Learning Leaves, the Story Stays

The Tuckman Model of Team Development is designed to help bring people together in ways that feel natural when forming groups. Everyone wants to be heard and play their part. We naturally gravitate to successful teams because they are a place where our potential can shine and we can refine our skills by listening to the ideas and experiences of other professionals.

My primary teaching duty at the medical school is to facilitate case-based learning teams. We practice team development both as instructors and with our student groups. The facilitators meet weekly to discuss updates, edits, or issues with the upcoming case. We follow the Tuckman Model, forming at the beginning of the semester, storming any new members of our facilitator group (not in a negative way—just getting them up to speed on the process), setting team norms that we all agree to abide by, performing throughout the semester, and ultimately adjourning for well-earned winter and summer breaks. Members of our faculty team bring their specialty to the table, including scientists, immunologists, physiologists, physicians, social workers, and medical humanists. Our model is a great way to share expertise to guide cases holistically for students, and it's also a lot of fun. We check in with any interesting happenings in either our professional or personal lives, getting to know our colleagues and building the trust necessary to navigate differences of opinion, and then we debrief how the session went at the end.

Using the Tuckman Model with students isn't very different. Our case-based learning sessions occur at the end of the week and the content mirrors what they learned in class during the week. Groups are made up of seven to nine students who remain together throughout the semester. We establish our team norms and schedule check-ins where the facilitator goes over a rubric with the students individually.

The things we talk about are what make the sessions special. The patients in each case are generally invented for the discussion, yet the students take pride in getting the diagnosis correct and sending the fictitious person on to a better life. They also feel the pain when someone does not follow the course of treatment or is diagnosed with a terminal disease. This environment allows students to practice their clinical skills, test their content knowledge, and consider what they would say to the patient if the case were real.

One of the most common norms that groups establish throughout the semester is that "learning leaves but stories stay." What that means is that we have to all be comfortable sharing our stories for the betterment of the group, which can be difficult if the group hasn't moved out of the norming or storming stage. The notion of "story stays" doesn't mean that the story is forgotten once the session ends; however, it is meant to assure everyone that our time together is a safe space in which to share personal experiences if we are comfortable. As such, I have found it helpful to share my own and my family's stories, as I feel they can help my students remember the importance of the human side of medicine. Sometimes it's as simple as what antibiotic my son was prescribed for a persistent ear infection or how long I had to keep my knee wrapped after having an old long jump injury scoped.

The experiences I share, however, aren't always so simple. One of the cases in our cardiology unit is about Tetralogy of Fallot, a rare congenital heart defect. This condition holds a somber meaning for me as I had a newborn daughter, Poppy, who passed away from the condition. Despite our doctors' best efforts, her little heart just wasn't meant for the world. When I saw the case on my schedule, I wasn't sure I was going to be able to teach it. But I decided I could handle it. It had been nine years since Poppy passed and I could share from my scars because they were no longer open wounds.

Despite my readiness, I was still nervous to share the story with the group. We had spent a few weeks together navigating the forming, storming, and norming stages. When I finished the story, the room was silent for a moment. I sensed their surprise followed by sadness. I had always been their support and suddenly I was the one who needed support. Then, a very thoughtful future physician responded with, "Thank you for sharing. I'm sure that was difficult but I appreciate how much you care about our learning." I was stunned, thanked her for her compassion, and reminded myself that I was there to facilitate their learning. I wondered if I had shared something too personal, but ultimately decided that sharing my painful story allowed the group to take a lesson with them (because "learning leaves") that was more illustrative than a chart on congenital heart defects.

We cover multiple body systems and clinical presentations throughout the semester and continue to grow in our knowledge and comfort with one another, but the adjourning stage of the Tuckman Model eventually arrives. How do you show appreciation for all the progress that has been made throughout a semester in a meaningful way? Well, the first step is pizza. In past semesters, I would buy pizzas and the students could bring whatever snacks and drinks they liked, but something still seemed to be missing. A large part of the storming and performing stages are based on feedback, so one semester I suggested, in addition to a pizza party on the last night of class, we also do a "secret Santa for feedback." The week prior I had students choose a slip of paper with someone else's name on it. I asked them to think about a positive affirmation they could give that person at the adjourning session. Secret Santa was a great success. Not only did team members adjourn with feedback they could take to their next team, but the students also decided to make it an actual Secret Santa, finding out from friends what their person liked and buying them a little trinket or snack. Most days, I really do love my job.

Chapter 8

Circle of Competence: Buffett and Munger

"I'm no genius. I'm smart in spots, but I stay around those spots."
—Tom Watson, IBM founder

If you ask someone to name a famous investor, more often than not, you're going to hear the name Warren Buffett. The "Oracle of Omaha" and his partner Charlie Munger worked together for over fifty years and turned Berkshire Hathaway into a multibillion-dollar company. At the core of their success is a seemingly simple principle: competence paves the path to success.[29]

Munger stated that competence can be a tricky concept, because it is relative to the individual. You may think you know what you're doing, but in reality, you are hopelessly lost. Or vice versa. You may be great at your craft but lack the self-confidence to realize it. In psychology, this is known as the Dunning-Kruger effect. Researchers David Dunning and Justin Kruger found that when people are asked to estimate their performance, they tend to regress to the mean.[30] Dunning and Kruger administered tests in areas like deductive reasoning, social skills, driving, and business sense and then asked the participants how they thought they did. Results showed that low performers overestimated their performance, while high performers underestimated theirs. The trend suggests that people tend to feel comfortable thinking they are average regardless of whether they are actually below average or above average. This research correlates to findings on other cognitive biases, such as high performers experiencing imposter syndrome, and low performers feeling inherently superior contrary to objective measures, a concept known as illusory superiority.

Buffett and Munger credit their success to what they call the Circle of Competence. According to their model, there are three important factors to identify when making a decision: what you know, what you think you know, and what you don't know. The core of your Circle of Competence is made up of the things you know. These are the facts (e.g., I have four employees; our goal is to create four widgets today). The next layer contains the things you think you know (e.g., I should have enough staff to accomplish our goal as long as no one calls off; my employees seem happy because they said so on our last staff survey). The third layer includes the nearly limitless things we don't know, such as market factors, competitors' strategies, or our colleagues' true feelings about a project.

Buffett says the most important characteristic of the Circle of Competence is not the size of the circle, but the awareness of the boundaries of each layer. What are the goals we know we can achieve right now? What are the goals we can achieve if the process unfolds as planned? Which goals are probably out of range? Success comes from hammering the items that fall within the core circle because they are the successes you can count on. The items in the "things you think you know" layer are achievable but not sure bets—they should be considered icing on the cake. Even if only a few suppositions from this middle layer come true, that should be considered a victory. Things outside the two inner layers are items that the decision-maker should be aware of but not try to control.

When explaining the Circle of Competence, Buffett often cites the 1986 book *The Science of Hitting* by Boston Red Sox Hall-of-Famer Ted Williams. In the book, there is a chart that shows Williams's batting average on pitches in different areas of the strike zone. A quick glance shows that a pitcher's best bet was to throw balls low and away to Williams. His batting average in those areas was in the low to mid 200s (out of a thousand). The spot to avoid was the high-middle range where Williams would hit in the high 300s. Ted Williams knew not only what pitches he liked, but he was acutely aware of his levels of competence.[31]

Buffett takes the Ted Williams hit chart very seriously. There is a picture of the chart in his office with Buffett's face superimposed over Williams. Buffett states that the Williams hit chart is even more useful in the world of investing because investing is a "no-called-strike" business. You don't have to move until you are ready and feel pretty secure that you are operating within your core of competence. Imagine how well Ted Williams would have hit if he didn't have to worry about the umpire calling him out.

Circle of Competence
Buffett and Munger

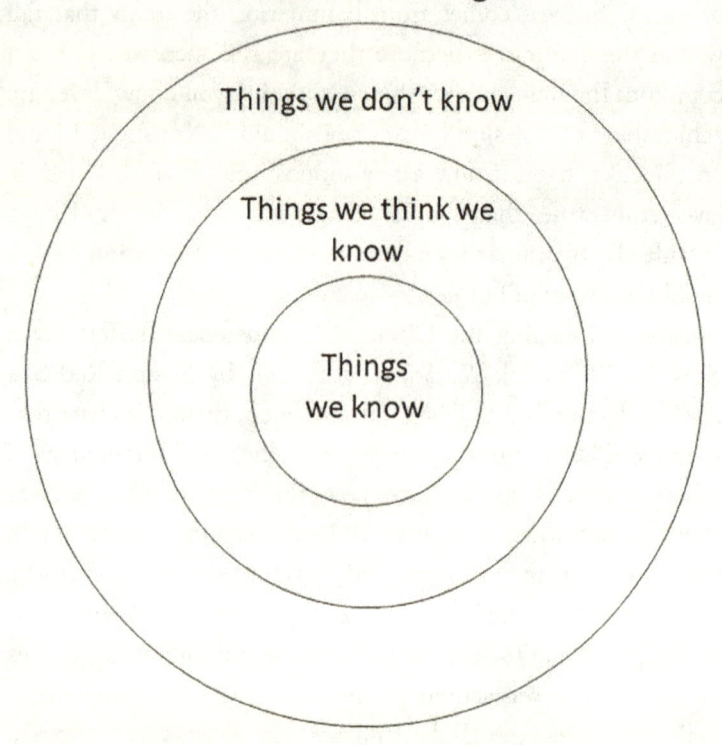

- Things we don't know
- Things we think we know
- Things we know

Bound for Cooperstown

The National Baseball Hall of Fame in Cooperstown, New York, has immortalized the Ted Williams's chart with a physical representation using colored baseballs to represent Williams's hot and cold zones. Although Cooperstown is one of my favorite places to visit—my wife and I go just about every year—I had not considered including its charm or curious history in this book until I came across Buffett's Circle of Competence and its ties to *The Science of Hitting*.

Cooperstown was founded in 1786 by William Cooper and was the boyhood home of his son James Fenimore Cooper, who grew up to be one of the most famous American authors of the nineteenth century, writing *The Leatherstocking Tales* and *The Last of the Mohicans*. But today, the town is most famous for being the birthplace of baseball, except for the fact that it isn't. Folklore asserts that Abner Doubleday invented baseball in a cow pasture (which is now a baseball field) and spread its popularity by teaching the game to Civil War soldiers while serving as a Union Major General. Baseball historians find the story dubious at best but agree it adds to the romanticism of the game; Cooperstown is therefore home to the Hall of Fame.[32]

I was twelve years old the first time I visited the Baseball Hall of Fame. I still have a throwback Mets #41 Tom Seaver jersey my mom bought for me. I wore it multiple times per week in the summer before eighth grade. As I learned on my most recent trip to Cooperstown, it still (mostly) fits, despite a few moth holes and a permanently creased collar (see the picture at the end of this story). One picture that the twelve-year-old me took on that first trip was of the "infield shift" for Ted Williams. That picture hung on my bulletin board throughout my adolescence.

For those who don't follow baseball strategy, an infield shift is when you move all but one infielder to a batter's pull side of the infield because they hit the ball to one side so often. The shift grew in popularity long after Williams stopped playing and gave such a strategic advantage to the defense that Major League Baseball banned it in 2023. While the shift was commonplace in the years leading up to it being outlawed, it was a strategic move used only against the greatest hitters when Ted Williams played, back in the 1940s and '50s. I loved the strategy of baseball as a kid and had never seen anything like the position of those players in that grainy black-and-white photograph. My infield shift picture was not unlike Buffett's hit chart. Not only were both related to Ted Williams but both served as constant reminders of excellence.

The question to consider here is, should you spend your time expanding your circle or refining and leveraging your existing competence? Buffett believes it is a wise idea to learn about the things that don't come naturally to you but one should focus primarily on the things that do. The hard part can be identifying areas to ignore or delegate to colleagues with different expertise. Buffett said that when he started, real estate was something he thought was in his core circle but it turned out to be something he didn't know as much about as he thought. Luckily for him and Munger, they figured out how to bring real estate into their core circle and Berkshire Hathaway flourished. They once tried their hand at retail sales but realized that industry was in the outer layer and they quickly pivoted.

Misidentifying the boundary between "what I know" and "what I think I know" can be risky but probably won't upend your entire operation. Perhaps you're a principal and you asked a teacher to take on one more class than they are comfortable with or you are a director who asked a salesman to take on one client over their normal load. These decisions aren't going to shutter your doors but they will likely lower that person's productivity. The real danger zone lies in the outer reaches of what you think you know. Promising promotions or greater staffing in hopes of boosting employee morale without securing the funds to do so or investing with anticipated gains can get you in big trouble quickly.

Circle of Competence: Buffett and Munger 53

So, if you're ever in Cooperstown, bask in the nostalgia and folklore of the quaint village and be sure to visit the Ted Williams spray chart at the Hall of Fame—while now thinking about Warren Buffett's Circle of Competence.

Wearing my Mets #41 Tom Seaver jersey in front of the Williams hit chart at the Baseball Hall of Fame.

Chapter 9

Cognitive Load Theory: Sweller

"We have become so obsessed by numbers and by bottom lines that beauty and truth have been knocked aside."

—Tom Hodgkinson

We're all familiar with those times when difficult things come easily, or when tasks that we can usually accomplish easily seem impossible. Cognitive Load Theory (CLT) aims to identify the limits of performance capacity to maximize capabilities. In 1973, evolutionary biologist Leigh Van Valen borrowed a page from Lewis Carroll's *Through the Looking-Glass* when he described the Red Queen Problem.[33] While in Wonderland, Alice is told by the Red Queen that she must run increasingly faster to win the race because "It takes all the running you can do to stay in the same place." This creates quite a conundrum, as it would seem impossible to run any faster than our fastest. Yet, the point is valid because if everyone is running at their fastest pace, then everyone would in fact stay in the same chronological place in a race. Applied to organizations, the Red Queen Problem alludes to the importance of innovation as a means of "running faster" to catch your competitors. But, how do you know when you've reached your maximum capacity and are in danger of breaking down? That's where Cognitive Load comes in.

The history of Cognitive Load Theory goes back to psychology's early understanding of the limits of memory. In 1956, George A. Miller introduced the idea of seven-plus-or-minus-two units as working memory capacity.[34] Miller theorized that people can reasonably remember seven things at once (minus two, if your memory isn't the greatest; plus two, if you have an excellent memory). It is believed this is why phone numbers are seven digits long. But what about those pesky area codes? If Miller were correct, most of us would struggle to remember the ten digits. Fellow psychologists Herbert Simon and William Chase outlined the concept of short-term memory which can be used to chunk similar items.[35] They did so by asking chess players to remember important sequences or moments that led to a swing in momentum. Players more accurately represented the entirety of a game by committing sequential highlights to memory. For this next example, please think back to landlines because cell phone numbers don't always follow the pattern. (If you don't know what a landline is, go ask your grandma.) Area codes are specific to a large region. The next three numbers are specific to a town or section of a city. By chunking, we can assume the first three digits and only need to remember the latter seven digits.

John Sweller attempted to build a new learning theory in 1988, expanding upon the work of researchers like Miller, Simon, and Chase, by finding the sweet spot of human cognition. He sought to find a means-ends analysis that would present the information needed to solve a problem without adding any extra frills that could confuse the student.[36] In a contemporary example, artificial intelligence programs attempt to do the same thing. They search the internet for everything they can find but only present what an algorithm tells them is most useful. Don't worry, Chat GPT isn't sentient . . . yet. Sweller defined a few different types of memory.

Sensory memory is the beginning of cognition. What do I hear around me? Where am I spatially? How do I physically feel? We don't process any of these stimuli into sensory memory until we make it a point to think about them.

Short-term or *working memory* comes next. This form of memory is whatever we are thinking about in a moment. Right now, I'm focused on writing about cognitive load and hopefully, you are thinking about cognitive load (unless you're daydreaming, more on that to come). However, the trick with working memory is that it is fleeting and limited. Multitaskers believe they can do multiple things at once. In actuality, they are skilled at task switching, the ability to quickly jump back and forth between thoughts in short-term memory.

Long-term memory has the greatest capacity; some researchers even believe long-term memory has unlimited capacity. But again, there's a trick. We have to commit the effort to move something from working memory to long-term memory. If one of my students wants to be a heart surgeon, they are probably jamming as much information as possible from the cardiology and hematology units into their long-term memory, whereas information about the endocrine or renal systems only sticks around in short-term memory long enough for the exam and then fades away. Once knowledge is committed to long-term memory, it can be acted upon in skill transfer.

Let's add a layer. Cognitive Load Theory also attempts to

explain our focus and capacity for learning in a way that makes it actionable. There are two types of cognitive load: intrinsic and extraneous.

The intrinsic cognitive load is the knowledge we are attempting to learn. Studying material for a test, learning a new software program, or figuring out how to compile budget reports are all examples of activities that fall into the intrinsic category.

Extraneous cognitive load is anything not related to learning that our brain is taking in. Too many words on a PowerPoint slide, overly detailed explanations, or charts and tables that present too much data at once are prime examples of common mistakes people make that detract from what we are trying to learn.

Cognitive overload is the experience of reaching the breaking point. I struggled with algebra in high school. By step four of most problems, I was hopelessly lost. Cognitive overload set in somewhere between my first misunderstanding and the next couple of steps. It's not that I couldn't understand algebra, it's that I needed the information broken down in a way that made sense to me. On the other hand, I excelled at history, but that doesn't mean I could absorb an entire book in one sitting. Our coworkers, especially those new to a field, may experience the same phenomenon. What they are comfortable with may come quickly but still has its limits. If they are struggling with a new concept, they are not failed hires or incapable; they may simply need more practice in ways that make sense to them.

Last but not least in Sweller's CLT is germane processing, defined as the effort it takes to process new information. Are we focused on what we should be focused on? If I've bored you and you're daydreaming, it's because your germane processing has flatlined. If you love this topic and can't wait to read the next line, your germane processing is spiking. Sports commentators will sometimes say athletes get "in the zone." When asked what "the zone" is, athletes struggle to explain it. Everything just slows down and the three-pointers start falling or the fastball leaves the pitcher's hand looking like a beach ball. What they are experiencing is a spike in germane processing known as "flow state." The athlete is keenly focused, their brain is channeling thousands of hours of practice, and what is normally difficult becomes automatic. But just like working memory, this spike is fleeting. A basketball player hitting every shot would require the same brain power it would take to remember every thought you had that day all at once.

Cognitive Load Theory
Sweller

Sensory Things going on in the background	**Intrinsic Load** Things we want to learn	**Cognitive Overload** Inability to process information
Short Term/ Working Thinking in the moment	**Extrinsic Load** Things distracting our learning	**Germane Processing** When tasks become automatic
Long Term Things committed to memory		

Decisions, Decisions

The Gömböc is a shape that shouldn't exist.[37] It looks similar to an egg with a curved bottom, flat sides, and a chunky top. What makes the Gömböc intriguing to mathematicians is that it has two states of equilibrium: one stable and one unstable.

To the average person, the Gömböc is interesting because it appears to have a life of its own. No matter what position a three-dimensional version of the Gömböc is put in, it will twist and roll until it finds that stable point of equilibrium. It is a shape that cannot rest until it knows its work is done.

Did that last line resonate with you? Do you identify with the Gömböc from time to time, not able to rest until you know your work is done? This is not an uncommon occurrence in an increasingly demanding work world. I couldn't finish our discussion of CLT without including a few words on reflection and self-care.

Nedra Glover Tawwab leverages the power of over one million Instagram followers to help spread mental health awareness through "bite-sized chunks." In her book *Set Boundaries, Find Peace*, she outlines strategies to keep sane by learning how and when to say no.[38] Our personal and professional lives ask so much of us that it's easy to put ourselves last; however, doing so creates an unsustainable pace and jeopardizes mental health. Tawwab takes this a step further and explores the real and perceived messages we communicate when we say no. Are we afraid of offending others when we tell them no? Are we afraid we'll be perceived as weak or lazy? What happens when too many "yeses" in our professional lives start to affect our relationships with friends and family? Taking care of yourself sounds like an easy proposition, but when life becomes a balancing act, we can lose sight of our own needs and be left to pitch and roll like our friend the Gömböc.

One way to strike a better balance is to consider productivity. Human performance researcher Sookyung Suh stated that Meaning plus Impact equals being Productive.[39] Productivity isn't how many reports you filed today, how many articles you publish in a year, or how many widgets you created on an assembly line. True productivity is the combination of what you find meaningful and its impact on those around you. I know that sounds very idealistic and I realize that passion doesn't always pay the bills. Nevertheless, passion projects are great for both leader and employee morale. It is the things we care the most about that build our professional expertise and ultimately build the company's reputation.

With that said, there is only so much time in a day and only so much thinking our cognitive load can handle, so we do need to prioritize. Whenever I think of prioritization, I think of the thirty-fourth President of the United States, Dwight David Eisenhower. Seriously, conjure up an image of Ike. Do you like President Ike or WWII Hero Ike? Either one will work. The reason I make this request is that the organizational management model known as the Eisenhower Decision Matrix goes back to Ike's philosophy on establishing priorities.

According to the matrix, if a task is urgent and important, do it now. If it is urgent but not important, consider delegating the task to someone who can help you. If it is important but not urgent, schedule a time to do it later. If it is not important and not urgent, is it something that has to get done at all?[40]

Everyone's brain is different and our situation affects our cognitive load daily. How did I sleep last night? Am I hungry? Does anyone else think it's cold in here? Why did I have that argument right before I left for work? Whether I'm fatigued due to long periods of focus or the influence of outside factors, often the simple solution is to take a break. Stand up and stretch, walk around the building, or grab a cup of coffee. These quick breaks won't necessarily bring about maximum cognitive load or prime germane processing but they help me refocus on the task at hand.

This is important information for leaders to practice personally and also with their employees. Consistently leading "like Ike" will help your employees keep their cognitive load in check. A leadership style that leans too far in the direction of the "Red Queen" runs the risk of overloading employees with more than they can cognitively process.

Chapter 10

Situational Leadership: Hersey and Blanchard

"Play better."
—Buck Showalter,
on inspirational quotes

Paul Hersey and Kenneth Blanchard introduced a new generation of the Leadership Continuum in 1982 called Situational Leadership. Like its predecessor, this theory supposes that the best leadership style corresponds to a balance of directive and supportive behavior based on an employee's readiness to complete assigned tasks independently. The two basic questions of Situational Leadership are: (1) How competent is your colleague (your perspective)? And (2) How confident are they in their abilities (their perspective)?[41]

Hersey and Blanchard's model is made up of Development Levels (D) and corresponding Leadership Styles (S).

D1 is low competence and high commitment. These

Situational Leadership: Hersey and Blanchard

employees are inexperienced but enthusiastic—think of someone just starting their first job. They're excited to get started but not sure what to expect.

D2 is low or some competence and low commitment. This is someone who is still developing the skills needed to complete job duties and for that reason is not yet able to accomplish the task.

D3 is moderate or high competence and variable commitment. This person has developed the skills required to succeed but perhaps lacks the confidence to do so consistently.

D4 is an employee who has fully developed. They have high competence and high commitment. These employees are self-reliant and need little to no direction to accomplish the task.

The corresponding Leadership Styles are as follows:

S1 is the Directing level. The leader is making decisions without consulting the team. At an extreme level, the leader maneuvers in an autocratic manner in which the decision is dictated and the team is expected to carry out the directive. The Directing level is similar to the *tells* and *sells* stages of the Leadership Continuum and the *Forming* stage of the Tuckman model.

S2 is the Coaching level. The leader defines the roles and tasks, is receptive to feedback, and trusts the team to execute the plan. Think of a sports team. The coach decides which players will work best in each position and makes adjustments as necessary, but doesn't actually play the game. The Coaching level is similar to the *suggests* and *consults* stages of the Leadership Continuum and the *Storming* stage of the Tuckman model.

S3 is the Supporting level. In this style, the leader is embedded in the team. The team decides what is best with the leader participating in the decision-making process as a near equal to everyone else. The Supporting level is similar to the *joins* stage of the Leadership Continuum and the *Norming* stage of the Tuckman model.

S4 is the Delegating level, in which the leader takes a laissez-faire approach, allowing the team to make independent decisions while providing minimal direction and guidance. This style is only appropriate when trust has been established. The Delegating level is similar both in name and action to the *delegates* stage of the Leadership Continuum, as well as to the *Performing* stage of the Tuckman model.

Situational Leadership
Hersey and Blanchard

	Development Level	Leadership Style
D1	Low competence/ High commitment	L1- Directing
D2	Low competence/ Low commitment	L2- Coaching
D3	High competence/ Variable commitment	L3- Supporting
D4	High competence/ High commitment	L4- Delegating

Ahhh . . . Spring

Spring is a time of rebirth, especially if you live in the Northeast. The snow melts, the grass goes from brown to green, and you start to see flowers peeking up through the earth. While I'm no fan of winter, living in an area of the country that experiences all four seasons does provide a natural rhythm that seems to flow more easily from year to year.

Even though the second academic semester of the year starts in January, which is still deep winter in the Northeast, "Spring" is the label given to this new semester. Students return from Winter Break to start a fresh set of classes. Many freshmen go home over the holidays and share brand-new ideas and outlooks with their parents and high school buddies. You somehow leave your hometown in August and return a changed person by December. That's the magic of education.

March brings baseball fans Spring Training in Florida and Arizona. For those of you who aren't fans, Spring Training is when all your players head to warmer weather and the manager gets their first look at the team as a whole. It is not uncommon for a thirty-million-dollar player to be batting just ahead of an eighteen-year-old international signee who is living in a team motel and adjusting to life in the US. This is the time when prospects get to show off their potential with the big boys. The stars of today's game know eventually they will become wily veterans and that the young men around them are the future. While there is no sure way to determine who will make it and who will flame out, every baseball prospect hopes to move from prospect, to star, to vet.

April brings exhibition games, during which I watch my beloved Mets knock off the rust in Port St. Lucie, Florida. This particular spring marks a milestone in our house. My wife is working on a doctorate; as I write this, she is a few months in and noticing how much she is beginning to view her profession in a different light. The day-to-day work somehow seems more micro; whereby, her theoretical studies are the juicy macro stuff that can change not only her work professionally but also herself personally. She asked if I experienced something similar when I was in graduate school. I told her I had and that it was a transformational experience.

Before this spring, I completed a narrative-based medicine class where a professor asked us to write a six-word biography. I chose, "My parents' child; my children's father." This seemed appropriate because the biggest progression in my life was from boy to man and man to father. But if I'm being honest, the second most impactful progression was the aforementioned August to December of that first year of college. I went from a kid in my hometown to a young man exposed to the world of academia and later a young professional introduced to the inner workings of that world. It's cool to share the latter experience with my wife as she takes the next step in her career.

At twenty-two, ink barely dry on my master's degree, I felt like the young prospect showing up at spring training. I was green, showed a lot of potential, and was most certainly a candidate for Hersey and Blanchard's Developmental Levels 1 and 2. I was enthusiastically full of ideas but lacked the practical knowledge of what a teacher actually did. I built confidence in the same way many teachers do. I volunteered for committees, agreed to advise clubs, and took on extra-curricular activities that I felt qualified to lead.

My success was a testament to hard work but also attributed to my school's principal for handling me with the correct Situational Leadership style, not unlike a Spring Training manager overseeing the development of a top prospect. He directed me when I was lost; he coached me up when I started building confidence. By my late twenties, I started to feel like I belonged, unknowingly cracking Developmental Level 3. The day-to-day operation of my classroom and the school became routine. There were certain projects that I was more passionate about than others (see "variable commitment"), yet I was moving from prospect to contributing player. I didn't feel like the star I wanted to be, but I was getting there. And again, my supervisor recognized my growth and took on an S3 Supporting style. He trusted me to help with interviews and mentoring new hires, my voice became a little more pronounced in committee meetings, and I was summoned to make presentations for school boards and at local conferences. I felt like a starter in the big leagues.

At this point in the story, you might expect me to say that I achieved Developmental Level 4 and my supervisor employed Leadership Style 4 and we all lived happily ever after. That, however, would not be true. I chose to reset my career in much the same way my wife is currently resetting hers. I'd enjoyed my thirteen years in K–12 education as a teacher and a leader, but it was time to do something new. No offense to my teacher friends, but I needed more, something that would fulfill my desire to do scholarship and have a larger academic voice. I was a D3 teacher (highly competent, variable commitment) who wanted to be a D1 professor (low competence, highly committed). My supervisor understood. He and I still catch up when our paths cross. He recently texted me at a soccer game and when I asked where he was, he replied with a picture of the back of my head as he was seated three rows behind me.

An ever-present career trajectory tends to just happen if all conditions are correct. I've heard an interesting rhetorical question concerning the development of a highly competent/highly motivated professional: When does a cucumber become a pickle? We dive into the jar a little bland and come out delicious, but there isn't a single moment when the transition occurs.

Many of my physician colleagues speak glowingly about the mentorship they received as they moved from medical student, to resident, to fellow, to attending. (Many people don't realize that it takes doctors on average ten to fourteen years to become fully licensed.) No matter what the field, the value of mentorship is crucial and we must recognize the leaders who help move us along the directive/supportive continuum. Leaders develop a generation of prospects into the superstars that ultimately one day replace them. No profession can advance without this transition. One spring, you're the hot prospect and everyone is looking to see if you're going to pan out. If you're committed to your craft, and a bit lucky, it's not too many more springs until you're hitting cleanup and signing that first big contract.

And before you know it, many springs have come and gone and others are looking to your expertise and wisdom. It's a great ride. Make sure you enjoy it.

Chapter 11

Four Frame Model: Bolman and Deal

"I need to think something lasts forever, and it might as well be that state of being that is a game; it might as well be that, in a green field, in the sun."

—A. Bartlett Giamatti

In 1984, Lee Bolman and Terrence Deal created an innovative theory on leadership called the Four Frame Model. As the name suggests, just about any organization can be viewed through four lenses, or frames. The first frame is Structural, whereby we consider rules, roles, and goals. The second is Human Resources, with a focus on optimizing individual skill sets to optimize overall performance. The third is Political, addressing conflict and competition. And lastly, the fourth frame is Symbolic, focusing on culture and meaning.[42]

Below are four short stories that illustrate each of Bolman and Deal's frames. Each can fall into numerous frames, depending on

Four Frame Model
Bolman and Deal

Structural roles, goals, policies	Human Resources needs, skills, relationships
Political power, conflict, competition	Symbolic culture, stories, meaning

Structural: The Toolbox

Psychologist Abraham Kaplan outlined the Law of the Instrument in 1964, stating, "Give a small boy a hammer, and he will find that everything he encounters needs pounding."[43] Kaplan's colleague Abraham Maslow furthered this notion in his 1966 work, *The Psychology of Science*. A quote commonly attributed to Maslow states, "If the only tool you have is a hammer, you tend to see every problem as a nail."[44] Both quotations illustrate an overreliance on a familiar tool. I often use a variation when discussing educational methods with colleagues. "When I see a nail, I want a hammer. When I see a screw, I want a screwdriver." The funny thing about coining your own pithy sayings is that they are rarely unique. When researching this section, I came across an old English saying, "Horses for courses," meaning trainers would be wise to select the correct racehorse for a specific track or weather. My toolbox analogy pretty much means the same thing.

Kaplan and Maslow are warning about overreliance on a favorite tool and the importance of seeing a task as it is. My suggestion would be to consider the task and determine if it is a nail or a screw *before* we reach into the toolbox. A tried-and-true lecture might be a bit outdated compared to more interactive forms of instruction; however, if laying a foundation of knowledge is the goal, then there isn't anything wrong with a short (operative word: short) lecture. I see a nail; where's my hammer?

However, if the task is more complex or time-consuming, a more refined tool may be required. I can hang siding with a hammer and nails in the same fundamental way as I can with a nail gun. It's just going to take forever. As an academic example, course evaluation data can be analyzed by hand (hammer/screwdriver) but it can be done more efficiently using a computer program like SPSS or NVivo (nail gun/power drill). When it comes to an organization, don't supply people with hammers if a truckload of screws is about to show up.

I spoke about the topic of choosing the right tool for the job at a technology education symposium a few years ago. A few days later, I received an email from an attendee interested in pursuing the analogy. He wondered, "Have you ever considered asking: What kind of house are you building?" This comment gave me pause. If the task is a lesson that requires a specific tool, then the course or curriculum is the whole damn house. The tools I select might be entirely different if I'm building a shed out back than if I'm building a home complete with electricity and plumbing. The Structural frame encourages leaders to choose the right tool for the minute-to-minute effort it takes to complete a job, while also considering the scope of what they hope to accomplish over the long term.

Human Resources: The Left Fielder

As any baseball fan will tell you, an ideal position player can both hit and play the field. In reality, this isn't always the case. Just about every Major League Baseball team has a player or two whose bat keeps him in the lineup, despite being a liability in the field. A manager can't hide more than one suboptimal glove at Designated Hitter (DH), so the outfield often becomes the area of give and take.

The center fielder must cover the most ground, as he doesn't have a foul line to his left or right. For this reason, the centerfielder is usually a fast runner with a good glove. This player usually doesn't have the strongest throwing arm, which is okay because the expectation is usually just to get the ball to an infielder after making the catch. The right fielder doesn't have to be as fast as the center fielder because he does have a foul line to his left. His job is to make sure nothing falls to his left and help cover the gap between right field and center field. This player, however, does have to have a strong throwing arm. The right fielder not only has to make the occasional throw to home plate, but he also has to make the long throw from right field to third base when a runner is trying to advance from second.

This brings us to the left fielder. No offense to any left fielders out there, but you're the extra guy. He is generally the guy who can hit, but may not be the most versatile defender or have the strongest throwing arm. When I presented this topic last semester, I asked a future physician who also happens to be a former college baseball player what positive attributes a left fielder possesses. Without pause he said, "The defense may not be there but he can hit the sh- crap out of the ball." I thanked him for holding his swear word. As my student illustrated, the left fielder guards the foul line to his right and helps in the gap between left field and center field. He'll have to make a throw home occasionally but rarely is a long throw necessary from left field to first base. Essentially, a left fielder is a failed right fielder.

But let's not be too harsh on the left fielder. Maybe he used to be an outfield dynamo, but Father Time caught up so he needs a place where he can age gracefully. Maybe he is a great hitter but is simply the second largest defensive liability (the greatest defensive liability would be DH). After all, Ted Williams was a left fielder. Both Barry Bonds and Rickey Henderson played out the later years of their careers as primary left fielders. The left fielder might have great value to the team, so the manager has to find ways to implement his strengths while limiting weaknesses.

So, who is your left fielder? Who on the team has 40-home-run potential, assuming they can be stowed in left field to accommodate their suboptimal defense? In organizations, we often focus on what a colleague can't do as opposed to what they could achieve if put in the correct situation. Every organization has lower performers. They might never hit leadoff or bat in 120 runs but a good leader might be able to increase their productivity by letting them play their game and finding ways to cover their limitations. It's a better option than waiting for them to leave or going down the messy road of terminating an employee who isn't necessarily doing anything wrong, but is just not doing enough things right.

Political: The Gloater

Every teacher's favorite part of the new school year is the morning of the first in-service day (sense the sarcasm?). This occurs a few days before the students return and usually the only thing on everyone's mind is, "Can we hurry this up? I have to get my room ready for the kids." Rosters, seating charts, decorations, welcome packets, and not-so-welcome packets full of picture day, contact card, and free lunch forms all have to be prepared. The morning in-service normally consists of a few words of welcome from the superintendent, introductions of new staff, a report on new happenings and yearly goals by the building principals, and perhaps a motivational speech if your district has the money.

One particular morning's agenda included a report from a central office administrator and a financial presentation offering 403b accounts for educators (this was not a school district that had funds for a motivational speaker). Teachers sat interspersed throughout the auditorium, mostly in loosely gathered grade-level or content-area teams. Things went swimmingly until the central office administrator took the stage. He had decided it would be a good idea to welcome the staff back by showing pictures of what he did during the summer. Innocuous enough, I suppose. Attempting to build rapport with staff, perhaps.

The problem was that he showed pictures of the pricey Hawaiian vacation and Alaskan cruise he and his wife went on, followed by candid shots of them at a conference in Japan. The room full of teachers was flabbergasted. A colleague near me said, not so quietly, "Are you f'ing kidding me?" in response to a picture involving martinis served in ice glasses that the administrator described as "neat." The climate in the room turned as icy as the "neat" Alaskan glasses.

I'm still not sure what the administrator had hoped to accomplish but the only outcome was alienating his entire staff. Most people in attendance that day were balancing taking a week-long family trip to the shore with paying their child's state school tuition bill. No teacher in the room had attended a professional development workshop outside the building in two years, let alone attend an international conference. The juxtaposition of the luxury lifestyle presented by the administrator with the presentation of a 403b plan that would help with the teachers' retirement funds—assuming they could afford to contribute—was painfully ironic. The gloater's lack of self-awareness was interpreted as braggadocio by the staff he was supposed to lead.

The simple lesson here is don't be the gloater. The more complex lesson is about navigating the Political frame. The administrator in this scenario created unnecessary conflict within the organization, blew vast amounts of political capital, and destroyed morale. Leaders usually earn more than their employees and, generally speaking, have earned that income through years of hard work. Gloating only alienates colleagues, even if it is done unintentionally. People in leadership positions need to be mindful of their words and actions. Employees are watching and looking for guidance. When times get tough, you want them behind you and not walking away.

Symbolic: The Town

Hardwick, Vermont, registered a population of three on the 1790 census and has never topped 3,200, except during the granite boom of 1910 when they made 3,201.[45] Despite the small population, the town boasts a few restaurants, a gift shop, a great coffee shop, a co-op, and a ton of history. The town's sense of community and its challenges have been documented by award-winning podcaster Erica Heilman (*Rumble Strip*) and local author Brett Ann Stanciu (*Unstitched*).

With all due respect to Front Seat Coffee and their amazing maple pastries, my favorite place in Hardwick is the Galaxy Bookshop. Nestled between a florist and a Chinese restaurant, the bookstore has a few stacks and a picture window, which also doubles as the domain of a mostly friendly feline. My wife, Katie, has been visiting there since she was three years old. In the summer of 2022, horrible news reached us in Pennsylvania that the apartment above the bookshop had caught on fire. I had never considered what happens to a first-floor bookstore when a second-floor fire requires mass quantities of water to save the building, but you won't be surprised to hear that all the books and bookshelves were ruined.

When Katie and I spent a few days at the family cabin a short drive from Hardwick, I dreaded walking up the main street to see the condition of Galaxy. The floors were bare. There were no shelves. The only item in the space was a new toilet waiting to be installed, which I took as a hopeful sign. They managed to reopen in January 2023, and local authors saw that the Galaxy reopened in style, with an informal celebration of intermittent guests, local food, and of course a few readings. I'm hoping that the first time the owners of Galaxy read this story is when this book sits on their shelves.

I could think of no greater example of the Symbolic frame than the reopening of the Galaxy: an independent bookstore in a municipality of less than three thousand that has managed to stay open since 1988, returning to glory after being completely destroyed because the community demanded it. What pillars hold up your organization in the same way in which having an independent bookstore supports the identity of Hardwick, Vermont? If suddenly ripped away, what aspect of your organization would spur an immediate need to regain it? That's your culture. That's your Symbolic frame.

Chapter 12

Transactional and Transformational Leadership: Bass

"A big part of teaching is mind over matter. Things you don't mind, probably don't matter."
—Bob

Although the term was coined earlier, Bernard Bass is the scholar most closely associated with Transformational Leadership. In his 1985 book *Leadership and Performance Beyond Expectations*, Bass defines Transformational Leadership as focused on influencing employees to work toward a shared organizational vision as opposed to what best serves their self-interests.[46] This theory stands in opposition to Transactional Leadership, in which the leader encourages individuals to complete a defined role in exchange for a defined reward. While Transformational Leadership is more person-centered from a holistic sense than Transactional Leadership, the best approach depends on the specific scenario. Transactional leaders tend to be focused on goals, use rewards as motivation, and react to what happens. This is similar to the Position of Power discussed in Fiedler's Contingency Model whereby the leader derives power from the ability to reward or punish performance. Transformational leaders focus on steady progress toward attaining a shared vision. This approach is less reactive and gives the team the choice of how to best achieve the ultimate goal. It doesn't ensure that mistakes won't happen but rather embraces mistakes as necessary steps in the process.

Transactional and Transformational Leadership

Bass

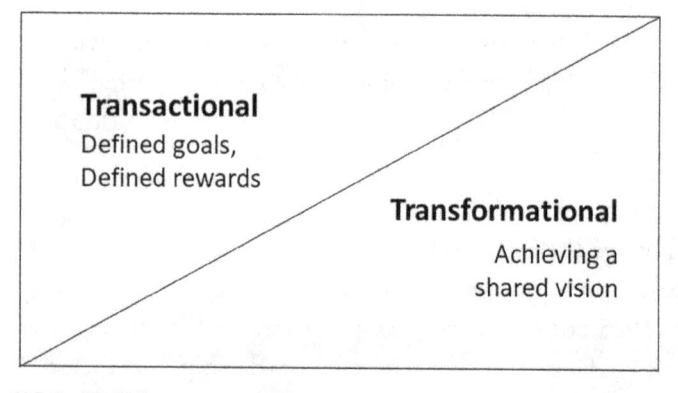

Transactional
Defined goals,
Defined rewards

Transformational
Achieving a
shared vision

Call Me "Bob"

I sat in an office, waiting for a man I'd never met, mulling over the idea of a master's degree that would prepare me to sit for the teacher licensure exam. I was set to graduate in a few weeks with a degree in history and philosophy. My plan was to pursue a PhD; however, teaching high school for a few years first seemed like a decent way to pay the bills. The chair of the history department had set up this meeting for me, but I was a little annoyed about the necessity of getting an education degree. To my mind, I knew history better than any of the education majors in my classes. Their grades were inflated by those "teaching courses." Meanwhile, I did the hard research and wrote the long papers, hours spent squinting at old newspapers on microfilm in the back of the library where other coeds snuck off to take a phone call or make out. I couldn't help but ask myself, *What am I even doing here?*

The man who sat across from me that spring day already had quite a career as a teacher, coach, administrator, and professor. The first thing most people noticed about Dr. Robert E. Gates (or Bob, as I would come to know him) was his thick Maine accent. He would often say, "You can tell who the out-of-towners are at a wedding. They order the lobster (pronounced *lob-sta*). Having steak is the treat for us." Bob had been an English teacher and basketball coach at Calais High School in Calais, Maine, before becoming a principal, and spoke fondly of his time there. He loved working with students and seeing them develop into productive adults. At the beginning of his career in Calais, not many students went to college; they were more likely to get married after high school and go to work at the Dexter Shoe factory, a staple of Maine's industry throughout the mid-twentieth century.

In Calais, Bob (known as "Mr. Gates" at his school) played a unique role as a leader. The local industry required that his style be more transactional than transformational, focused on vocational demand and opportunity. Kids were asked to perform tasks based on developmental appropriateness, moving from grade to grade and ultimately earning a high school diploma. They did well in class and learned to function as a team. Their reward at the end of four years was a consistent job that provided a comfortable middle-class existence. Again, this wasn't the case for all students. Top scholars went to college, some never to be heard from again while others returned home to contribute to the community where they grew up.

Bob left Maine to pursue a doctorate from the University of Louisville and eventually landed a job as a professor at Bloomsburg University, where our meeting took place. He was chair of the education department and well-liked by students, staff, and other faculty members. I was once told during a job interview, "Dr. Gates must be really popular because every Bloomsburg candidate has a letter of recommendation from him." He had a gentle nature and focused on developing students into teachers. His philosophy was a simple exercise in proportions. Content knowledge is a third of what you need to be a good teacher. Teaching skills and "everything else" (managing students, communicating with parents, collaborating with other teachers and administrators, advising, coaching, etc.) make up the other two-thirds. Those other two-thirds need to be developed just as diligently as your knowledge of content.

As is the case in many good mentor/mentee relationships, I had unrealistic ideas of the profession at the start, and Dr. Gates was patient enough to listen to my theory that I would secure a teaching job without the proper licensure. "While it's possible to get a teaching job without a license," he said, "you would have to be the only applicant. The state won't allow a district to hire any unlicensed teacher over a licensed one." *Fine*, I thought, *let's get me into grad school*. Over the next eighteen months, I completed my master's degree.

The next dozen years of my professional life were spent honing my skills as a teacher and developing a passion for working with students. During those years, Bob became the dean of the graduate school at Bloomsburg, which offers a wide variety of graduate degrees in the fields of business, science, education, reading, information technology, nursing, and social work. The dean of this department must take a more transformational approach. Each academic department has its own set of values and needs. In an environment of limited resources, departments tend to compete with one another to secure enrollment and thrive. The dean must do their best to encourage everyone to work toward the vision of the university, as opposed to their department's self-interests. Bob excelled at this tedious balancing act.

We kept in touch and I occasionally reached out for professional guidance, although it took me a while to get used to calling him "Bob," as he instructed me, instead of "Dr. Gates." When I told him I was considering a doctorate, he encouraged me to do so not only because I was capable but because I would influence the lives of so many more people as a professor. He said, "A high school teacher will work with maybe one hundred kids per year for thirty years. That's three thousand. If you train teachers for thirty years and if even half of them have thirty-year teaching careers, think of all the lives you've touched." That equation resonates even more for me now that I have been given the opportunity to train future physicians who will deliver babies, counsel patients, and perform life-saving surgeries.

Five years after that doctorate conversation, I was told to wait outside in the hall while the dissertation committee discussed whether I had successfully defended my dissertation. Dr. Gates was sitting in the hall, fresh off a plane, waiting for me with a congratulations card in hand. It would have been a total bummer had I not passed. I had invited him but didn't anticipate he would come. In fact, he was the only one there. My kids were too young, my mom was taking care of my dad who would pass away a few short months after his son became a doctor, and I was divorced and unattached. But in retrospect, I wouldn't have had it any other way. The man who believed in me and started my journey into the field of education was with me at the end of one path and the amazing beginning of another.

Chapter 13

Appreciative Inquiry: Cooperrider and Srivastva

"Life moves on and so should we."
—Spencer Johnson, *Who Moved My Cheese?*

In most chapters, I have partnered a theory with a story, and I do the same here. Appreciative Inquiry is a leadership theory

Appreciative Inquiry
Cooperrider and Srivastva

- Discover: What is it?
- Dream: What could it be?
- Design: What should it be?
- Destiny: What will it be?

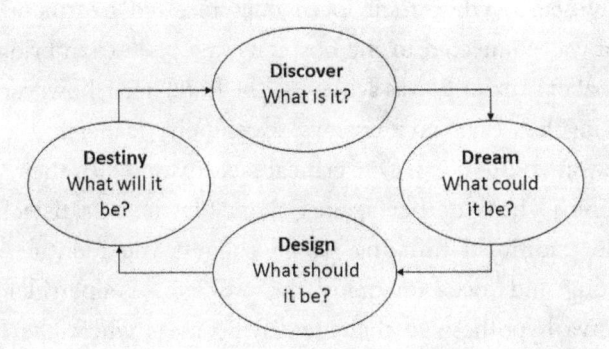

that came about through the unfolding of a great story. David Cooperrider was maybe the most overly ambitious doctoral candidate in the history of the academy. With his advisor Suresh Srivastva, Cooperrider set out to analyze organizations through a positive approach that focused on how to accentuate strengths, as opposed to remedying problems, a negative approach that he considered to be driven by fear. According to the theory of Appreciative Inquiry, organizations have a positive core, made up of attitudes, practices, and past successes that all add up to future successes. Cooperrider identified the four Ds of Appreciative Inquiry as: discovery (What is it?), dream (What can it be?), design (How do we achieve the dream?), and destiny (What has it become?).[47]

But back to the story. What became of Cooperrider's 1985 dissertation, "Appreciative Inquiry: A Methodology for Advancing Social Innovation," began at Case Western Reserve University in Cleveland, Ohio. Cooperrider and Srivastva approached the Cleveland Clinic about evaluating a targeted component of the healthcare leader's organization. The opportunity they identified was the Omni Hotel, which had been purchased by the clinic as a welcoming place for families to stay nearby while their loved ones received treatment. The Omni was connected to the hospital via a pedestrian bridge so the goal of proximity was achieved. The hotel itself, however, was receiving less than rave reviews. Hospitality leadership at the clinic was confounded. One critical factor worked in their favor (proximity) but another against them (customer satisfaction). While traditional thinking would suggest you identify what is wrong and focus on fixing the problem, Cooperrider and Srivastva hypothesized that identifying areas where the hotel could make realistic positive changes would resolve the negative.

The staff of the Omni were taken to a five-star hotel in Chicago and instructed to take notes on what the hotel did well and what made them feel welcomed. The notes allowed the staff to consider what a "fancy hotel" in a "big city" does. The staff then reflected on what they could reasonably recreate at their hotel, given the resources at their disposal. The goal wasn't to make the Omni a five-star, Chicago-style hotel, but to make the Omni as good as it could be by focusing on its positive qualities. Over time, the employees took more ownership of their hotel and made gradual consistent changes. The Appreciative Inquiry experiment was a success because leadership focused on opportunities for things to go right instead of worries about what could go wrong. Visitors to the Omni continued to appreciate the proximity to the hospital but also steadily reported a better experience. The hotel achieved its goal of giving families a nice place to stay during a stressful time. The Omni was torn down in the year 2000 but not because it was a failure. Today, a new InterContinental hotel on the same site serves Cleveland Clinic families and visitors to Cleveland alike.

Cooperrider obviously earned his PhD and continued to refine Appreciative Inquiry. He has written nearly twenty books on the subject and is the namesake of the David L. Cooperrider Center for Appreciative Inquiry at Champlain College in Burlington, Vermont. At its core, Appreciative Inquiry starts with collaboration, honest introspection, and sharing positive ideas about an organization, and only then looks for opportunities to succeed. Great things can happen when the focus stops being about fixing what is wrong and turns to accentuating what is right.

What Would You Do if You Weren't Afraid?

We have already established that I did not train to work at a medical school. I planned to complete a doctorate, buy a bunch of tweed jackets with corduroy elbow patches, maybe take up smoking a pipe, and be the stereotypical college professor for the thirty years or so that I still had to work before retirement. Despite that solid plan, there I was: thirty-five years old, a new doctor looking for a tenure track appointment, zero tweed jackets. Higher education jobs were as hard to find as decent pipe tobacco, especially for someone who had just graduated and had an existent but not very impressive record of research. When offered a job in academic affairs at a medical school, I figured, why not?

Every industry has its own jargon, and academic medicine is no different. The first conundrum I faced was the difference between undergraduate medical education (UME) and graduate medical education (GME). Undergraduate to me meant earning a bachelor's degree; graduate was a master's and higher, but I wasn't sure if that would be true of my students. I didn't want to ask anyone I worked with directly because that would confirm that I had no clue what the hell I was doing, so I asked an administrator at one of our clinical sites during a visit. She responded with, "Good question. Generally, med students are UME and residents are GME." Ok, that made sense. The site supervisor looked down her nose at me and asked if I had ever read *Who Moved My Cheese?* I told her I knew the gist but had not read the book, still faking like I was totally in control. She responded with, "You should," which sounded a bit menacing. I smiled, sipped my coffee, and walked away.

One of the bestselling business books of all time, Spencer

Johnson's *Who Moved My Cheese?*[248] examines themes of organizational complacency and innovation. Two mice and two "little people," who are the size of mice but act like people, live in a maze. Varying amounts of cheese show up in different places throughout the story and ultimately, the brave succeed while the apprehensive fail. In one of the more meaningful parts of the book, one of the people/mice finds the phrase "What would you do if you weren't afraid?" written on a wall in the maze. That question is a hallmark of Johnson's story and the one you are reading right now.

I hope my students know how much inspiration I draw from them. (Well, I guess they do now if they are reading this book!) Every one of them is remarkable. Our school routinely receives over five thousand applications for roughly one hundred and fifteen spots. You truly are the best of the best if you've made it to medical school. One of the students from our medical humanities club, Haydn, agreed to record a personal story for the *Journeys to Medicine* podcast I produce in conjunction with the club. She decided on a funny story about trying out for an acapella group without much musical training or, admittedly, talent. The group performed at freshman orientation and she was so intrigued by the beauty of the music that she wanted to be a part of the magic. In her story, she referred to an inspirational poster that hung at her undergraduate university. The poster read, "What would you do if you weren't afraid?" The phrase rang a bell for me but it wasn't until I decided to include her story in this book that I realized it was the line from *Who Moved My Cheese?*

Haydn left freshman orientation with the date for acapella tryouts and started planning. She wanted something classic but not too old, something soulful but not with a wide vocal range, as she didn't want to be overly ambitious. She settled on the 1993 hit "No Rain" by folksy rockers Blind Melon. Haydn practiced the song over and over for her roommates who politely encouraged her to chase her dream. On the big day, she entered the room to find a few members of the acapella group and a piano, on top of which was a box of assorted donuts. "Why is there a piano?" Haydn thought to herself. She quickly found out as members of the acapella group asked her to match pitch, striking a key. She didn't know how. They said that was okay and moved on to the song portion of the tryout. Haydn proudly told them she would be performing "No Rain." They didn't know the song. How can anyone who loves music not know the song with the bee girl in the video? As her nerves grew, the group members silently encouraged her and she got through the song. A little embarrassed but otherwise unscathed, she thanked them. They thanked her and told her to take a donut.

Haydn didn't make the acapella group, but she still remembers the tryout as a positive experience. Everyone was very polite and accommodating, plus they gave her a donut. I didn't get an assortment of tweed jackets but I found my academic home where people appreciate my ideas and encourage me to do silly things like write short stories about mobile cheese and '90s grunge classics to illustrate my academic pursuits. Haydn didn't get to sing acapella but she learned a lot from the experience. Our overlapping stories illustrate the lesson that you have two choices on the path to success: (1) Only do the things you know you will succeed at and never grow, or (2) Try everything with the goal of success but know that failure is a possibility. You'll never grow if you never step out of your comfort zone. However, as Buffett and Munger taught us earlier, be aware of how far you venture from your Circle of Competence.

Always playing it safe provides a stifling false sense of success. To paraphrase the inspirational words of Haydn: "be confident and take action even when you're nervous. Nervous about getting something wrong, nervous about looking foolish, nervous about failing. You might embarrass yourself but it won't be the first time or the last. Ask yourself what you want to do, remove fear from the equation, and go out and do what you love. Who knows? You might even get a donut."

Chapter 14

The Leadership Challenge: Kouzes and Posner

"We do not learn from experience . . . we learn from reflecting on experience."

—John Dewey

If you'll forgive the cliché, it has been said that great leaders are made, not born. I would agree with that statement, as would James Kouzes and Barry Posner who wrote, *The Leadership Challenge: How to Make Extraordinary Things Happen in Organizations*. First published in 1987, the seventh edition was released in 2023 with the authors continuing to refine their findings, which span more than thirty years of asking the question: "What do leaders do when they are at their personal best?" Kouzes and Posner took the above cliché a step further and asserted that not only are leaders made and not born, but leadership itself is a practice and not a personality.[49]

The two hallmarks of the Leadership Challenge are: (1) the most common characteristics of effective leaders and (2) the

The Leadership Challenge: Kouzes and Posner

Five Practices of Leadership, which include the Ten Behavioral Commitments of Leaders.

Although they compiled an extensive list over thirty years, Kouzes and Posner found that the four most common characteristics of effective leaders were that they were honest, forward-looking, competent, and inspiring. More important than ambition was simple honesty. More important than trailblazing was simple competence (think Buffett and Munger). A leader should be inspiring but doesn't have to be a motivational dynamo, and having a vision for success is more important than striving to be the absolute best. Sometimes outside pressures and competition get the best of us and we view anything less than achieving lofty goals as a failure. In actuality, all our colleagues want is a person who cares about them and has a vision for continued success. For many leaders, the tricky part of this is that you must be willing to set aside your pride. The Leadership Challenge can only be achieved through honest reflection about your idea of success, and the ability to consider compromise if required.

Kouzes and Posner's Leadership Challenge is a prime example of a longitudinal behavior-based study of leadership. Their work is often used as the basis for Authentic Leadership Theory. Several authors have attempted to define Authentic Leadership, which is why it is not included in this handbook; however, the collection of ideas includes topics such as trust, transparency, self-awareness, and integrity.

Leadership Challenge
Kouzes and Posner

Practice 1: Model the Way -finding your voice -setting the example	**Practice 2:** Inspire a Shared Vision -envisioning the future -enlisting others to create common goals
Practice 3: Challenge the Process -seeking ways to grow, change, and improve -experimenting, taking risks, and learning	**Practice 4:** Enable Others to Act -fostering collaboration -empowering others

Practice 5: Encourage the Heart
-recognizing the contributions of others
-celebrating values

The Five Practices and the Ten Commitments

Each of the Five Practices of Leadership identified in the Leadership Challenge is made up of two of the Ten Behavioral Commitments of Leaders.

Practice 1: Model the Way

A leader models the way by practicing the commitments of *finding their voice* and *setting the example*. The leader must reflect upon their actions and commit to the behaviors that they wish to see in their employees. Engaging in honest reflection and then sharing those insights with employees can build trust and foster positivity. A leader who is self-aware and genuine will attract like-minded followers.

Practice 2: Inspire a Shared Vision

A leader inspires a shared vision by *envisioning the future* and *enlisting others to create common goals*. By developing a set of goals that everyone understands and wants to pursue, the organization strives to achieve a big goal through a series of small steps. Working toward a shared vision is exciting and can promote innovative thinking.

Practice 3: Challenge the Process

A leader challenges the process by ***seeking ways to grow, change, and improve,*** and by ***experimenting, taking risks, and learning.*** Focusing on a growth mindset allows for the creation of more productive patterns, or, where possible, wholesale improvements. Colleagues are free to question unproductive behaviors and try new ideas. In this environment, it is safe to fail in the name of getting better.

Practice 4: Enable Others to Act

A leader enables others to act by ***fostering collaboration*** and ***empowering others.*** Employee expertise is focused on the job; leader expertise is focused on the organization. The leader is tasked with creating a safe environment for employees to do the work that they feel will be most impactful, thus avoiding micromanagement. The leader must turn over a level of control by admitting and accepting that their expertise is suited to the whole of the project and not the individual jobs that lead to the project's collective success.

Practice 5: Encourage the Heart

A leader encourages the heart by ***recognizing the contributions of others*** and ***celebrating values.*** To encourage the heart, leadership needs to genuinely celebrate successes and make people feel valued. We're not talking cake in the boardroom, but rather tangible rewards that create a culture where employees feel a sense of ownership of the organization's success. Tradition and history establish symbols and stories of success that transcend projects and create a history and legacy for the organization. Kouzes and Posner state that this is the most easily overlooked of the Five Practices but could be the most important to long-term success.

A large portion of the Leadership Challenge asks leaders to be honest with themselves. It is important to reflect upon routines and how they shape the organization. What blind spots might be present in your leadership style, based on your personality or professional experience? Answering this question shifts the focus from personal characteristics to the actions and skills of the person. Having these tough conversations with yourself and implementing healthy interventions helps leaders better understand their role and gain a clearer sense of self.

Chapter 15

Adaptive Leadership: Heifetz, Linsky, and Grashow

"I never lose. I either win or learn."
—Nelson Mandela

Ronald Heifetz outlined what would become Adaptive Leadership in his 1994 book, *Leadership Without Easy Answers*.[50] The theory was refined and expanded upon until Heifetz collaborated with Marty Linsky and Alexander Grashow on the 2009 work, *The Practice of Adaptive Leadership: Tools and Tactics for Changing Your Organization and the World*.[51] Adaptive Leadership is unique in that it is a model that isn't a model. Let me explain. In organizations, change is the only certainty. Therefore, an effective leadership model would define strategies for dealing with continual change, which is what Adaptive Leadership attempts to achieve. This is similar to Fiedler's Contingency Model where the best action was the best adaptation to change.

According to Heifetz, there are two types of tasks: technical and adaptive. Technical tasks are clearly defined and performed by someone with expertise. The goal when completing technical tasks is efficiency. Think of your family doctor's office. You arrive at your appointment, the receptionist checks your insurance information, you see the doctor, and they bill your insurance. The office operates efficiently. Everyone gets paid. You receive the care you need. Everyone is happy. In contrast, adaptive tasks are hard to define or not clearly understood. No single person has expertise in these tasks, and therefore, the goal becomes problem-solving. Let's use the same example as above. Maybe your family doctor's office is overrun with patients (some without insurance, which can complicate matters further) and the health system cannot provision additional providers. A long-term solution to this problem could be to focus on preventative medicine and patient education. There would be less demand for the doctor if the local population took better care of themselves or if they knew when a doctor's appointment is and is not necessary. Achieving this goal would require the input of many stakeholders beyond the doctor and their patients, such as community leaders, marketing specialists, and educators. The task is adaptive because it isn't clearly defined and no single person in this scenario has the expertise to resolve it by themselves. It is well worth the effort, however, as it creates a solution for everyone involved.

Additionally, leaders practicing Adaptive Leadership are either *exercising authority* or *exercising leadership*. Exercising leadership helps the team achieve adaptive tasks, and includes identifying and interrupting unproductive patterns. These leaders seek out new solutions, implement change, and adapt to a changing marketplace. While you may always want to operate in leadership mode, exercising authority has its place. When exercising authority, the leader provides direction by clarifying roles, protects the organization's scarce resources by minimizing vulnerability, and ensures order and stability. Not surprisingly, this top-down style is effective when the goal is efficiently completing technical tasks.

Adaptive Leadership places a premium on balancing interaction and reflection. The leader must observe the behavior of their colleagues so that they can appropriately intervene when necessary. Collecting workable data requires interaction while synthesizing and responding to those data requires reflection. The goal of Adaptive Leadership is to find what is called the Productive Zone of Disequilibrium (PZD). If the organization is overly technical, work becomes stagnant. If the tasks are overly adaptive, the constant flux of the workplace becomes chaotic. The perfect balance where the two overlap is the PZD.

Adaptive Leadership
Heifetz, Linsky, and Grashow

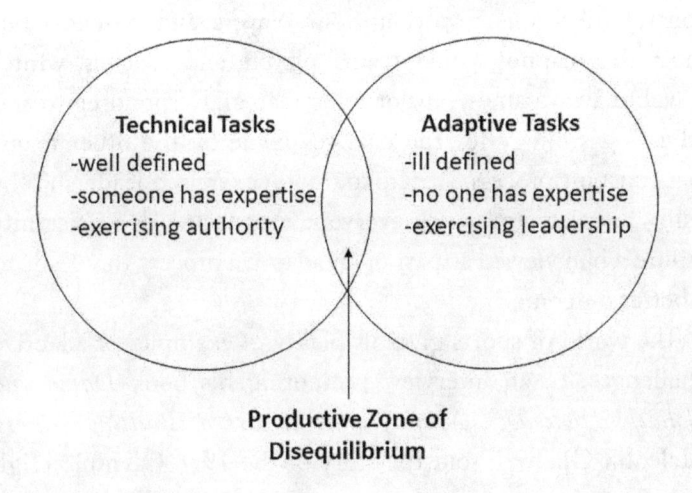

Technical Tasks
- well defined
- someone has expertise
- exercising authority

Adaptive Tasks
- ill defined
- no one has expertise
- exercising leadership

Productive Zone of Disequilibrium

Winning and Losing

In a 2021 *Harvard Business Review* article, Scott Edinger pointed out something that we all know but many of us find hard to accept, namely, that you can't fight reality. If things aren't going well, you can either waste a lot of time, effort, and energy trying to fix a losing proposition or adapt to the reality that is right in front of you.[52] Losing hurts but it's more palatable when viewed as progress and not failure.

As I touched up another section of this book, I heard a post-game comment made by basketball superstar Giannis Antetokounmpo that was making headlines. His top-seeded Milwaukee Bucks had just been eliminated by the bottom-seeded Miami Heat 4-1 in the first round of the 2022 NBA Playoffs. When asked if the season was a failure, Antetokounmpo said, "There's no failure in sports. You know, there's good days, bad days. Some days you are able to be successful, some days you're not."[53] Winning an NBA championship is an adaptive task. There are many moving parts, some of which a team can control (decisions regarding your players and coaches) but most they cannot (other teams' players and coaches, winter travel to away games, fans of other teams). Responding to and adjusting strategy for the changes made by the other teams is a constant process. Antetokounmpo exercised leadership by using his platform to tell everyone that losing doesn't signify failure when viewed as part of an adaptive process that leads to a better outcome.

The world of sports gives us plenty of examples of adaptive challenges. In an interview promoting his book *David and Goliath: Underdogs, Misfits, and the Art of Battling Giants*, Malcolm Gladwell told the story of the 1976 Olympic High

Jump. In 1976, Gladwell was thirteen years old and thrilled by the opportunity to watch the Montreal Olympics in his home country. His favorite athlete in those Olympics was American high jumper Dwight Stones. By the end of his career, Stones would win nineteen national titles and hold the world high jump record on three separate occasions. In 1976, however, he was a twenty-two-year-old looking to win his first Olympic gold, having finished with a bronze four years earlier. If the high jump were composed only of technical tasks, Stones would have won handily. He could jump higher than the other competitors and his form was impeccable. He was Goliath. He couldn't be beaten unless an unfortunate adaptation reared its head. For Stones, the adaptive challenge was rain. Granted, the other competitors had to jump in overcast and wet conditions as well, but Stones preferred dry conditions when he jumped. Stones unsurprisingly cleared the highest jump of the day (seven feet) but missed it once. Two other competitors cleared it on every attempt, forcing Stones to settle for his second consecutive bronze medal. It would appear Goliath was defeated by the rain.

Gladwell's book provides nine examples in which someone with what appeared to be an obvious advantage fell to the underdog, the most famous being the biblical epic of the title.[54] He presents a compelling argument that it was David who had the advantage that day in the Elah Valley. Goliath, a behemoth equipped with bronze armor and multiple weapons, anticipated the technical task of hand-to-hand combat. But David's ability to strike from a distance was an adaptation that played in his favor. After all, a sling coupled with the correct kind of rock in the hands of a shepherd used to slaying wolves and bears would have been deadly accurate. Goliath's folly was the ancient world's equivalent of "don't bring a knife to a gunfight." So is it really that surprising that David slew Goliath?

Recall the "horse for courses" analogy from Bolman and Deal's Structural Frame, an idiom I have adopted as my professional mantra. Hanging on the wall in my office is a framed 11 x 14 photo of a 1970s superstar much different than Dwight Stones. Secretariat was the greatest racehorse to ever live, having won the 1973 Triple Crown including the Belmont Stakes, the final leg, by an absurd thirty-one lengths. The picture of Secretariat (signed by jockey Ron Turcotte because I couldn't resist) reminds me that one horse who can handle all courses is exceptionally rare. A horse that can beat all the other best horses in the world by thirty-one lengths is pretty much impossible. Given his skill, racing became a technical task for "Big Red." Turcotte made sure Secretariat got off to a good start and the horse took care of the rest.

The story of Secretariat reminds me to revisit the notion of accepting reality. Antetokounmpo accepted that his Milwaukee Bucks didn't win the championship in 2022, but he could still relish in the memory of their 2021 championship that included his NBA Finals MVP recognition. Stones would never win Olympic gold but he is considered one of the greatest high jumpers to have ever lived. Secretariat did win the first Triple Crown in twenty-five years and retired to Claiborne Farm where he delighted visitors until his death in 1989.

You can be the most technically prepared and the most talented but sometimes unexpected adaptations get in the way just as they did for Antetokounmpo in 2022 and Stones in 1976. As

Edinger stated in his article, you don't have to be happy about it but acceptance gives you the power to move forward in the most effective way possible. I'm not Secretariat, Dwight Stones isn't Secretariat, Giannis Antetokounmpo isn't Secretariat, and you probably aren't either. Stones accepted reality at the Montreal Olympics and in early August 1976, less than a week after defeat, he set a new world record—jumping in dry conditions of course.

Chapter 16

Resonant Leadership: Goleman, Boyatzis, and McKee

"Unpleasantness is part of the experience."
—Barbara Heffernan, of Mindful Psychotherapy, on self-reflection

Returning to Daniel Goleman, the psychologist and father of Emotional Intelligence, we find that he theorized that leaders act as an emotional contagion. In fact, Goleman found that 50–70 percent of a team climate can be attributed to the leader's behavior.[55] Couple that with the statistic that 20–30 percent of team performance is tied to climate (also Goleman) and it becomes clear that emotions and teamwork have a great effect on outcomes. When in a group setting, our brains instinctually try to determine a hierarchy. We look to who is in charge and tend to focus on the verbal and nonverbal communication displayed by that person. (And don't discount nonverbal communication:

the psychology community believes that 70–93 percent of all communication is nonverbal.) As hard as it may be to admit, people are hardwired to focus just a little bit more on the pleasure or displeasure of their bosses than their day-to-day coworkers.

If you went to college, you probably sat in the big lecture hall or auditorium for Psychology 101, as most undergrads find that course listed for their general education requirements. I recall being taught that when faced with conflict, human beings will assess the situation and enter into either a fight or flight mindset. Am I in danger? Should I fight my way out or run like hell? Later in life, I was introduced to the third option: freeze. The advent of YouTube allowed many of us to view videos of people attempting to bungee jump or skydive whose brains would simply not let them jump. Sure, they were scared, but they wanted to jump, to feel the rush of an all-things-considered safe freefall. Yet there they were, looking into the camera saying, "I can't. My knees are locked."

Even more recently, I learned there is a fourth response to conflict: fawn. When a student submits a paper to their professor, they enter into a negotiation with an inherent power imbalance. Ideally, the student's primary goal is learning, but they also want to impress the professor. The desire to gain the professor's approval may instinctually activate a fawn response. This is a prime example of Goleman's emotional contagion at play.

Goleman has worked with Richard Boyatzis and Annie McKee on Resonant Leadership which can be broken down into four styles: Visionary, Coaching, Affiliative, and Democratic.[56]

Resonant Leadership
Goleman, Boyatzis, and McKee

Visionary	Affiliative
-big picture -ability to articulate the desired outcome without telling people what to do	-relationship building -requires self-awareness, emotional intelligence, and empathy
Coaching	**Democratic**
-developing talent -relies on trust, rapport, and encouragement	-investment in the process -considering everyone's vantage point even if the leader makes the decision

In the Visionary style, the leader can see the big picture. They have access to all the pieces that must fit together to achieve the desired outcome. When implementing the Visionary style, the leader can articulate how the group will achieve the desired outcome while remaining in an assisting role, without telling employees what to do.

In the Coaching style, the leader fosters the personal development of colleagues, usually in a one-on-one setting. Coaches build trust and rapport in part by encouraging colleagues to pursue passion projects. The successful completion of a passion project can both build employee satisfaction and bring positive attention to the organization.

The Affiliative style prioritizes listening, collaboration, and relationship-building. Achieving this demands the leader practice high levels of self-awareness, emotional intelligence, and empathy. The goal of the Affiliative style is to boost morale by valuing colleagues' contributions and feelings.

And lastly, the Democratic style draws on the knowledge of

the group to collaboratively make decisions. Employing this method helps the leader ensure that employees are invested in the process. The final decision may not be the decision that every employee had hoped for, but having their vantage point considered shows them that they are respected and valued by the leader.

A term often associated with Resonant Leadership is mindfulness. Mindfulness seems to be everywhere. Just the other day, I was in line at the grocery store and staring back at me was a magazine promising inner peace and stress relief if I followed the teachings within. As with most supposed life hacks, there's a much bigger story than what you can take home from the checkout line for $5.95.

Memory of the Present

In the Buddhist tradition, mindfulness begins with the word "sati" meaning "memory" in the Pali language. English speakers took the notion of sati and translated it to "mindfulness," or "to remember to observe." Mindfulness is the first factor of the Seven Factors of Awakening. One must be mindful or able to maintain awareness before they can progress toward enlightenment. The Seven Factors of Awakening go a little something like this. Awareness leads to an investigation of reality. Investigation takes effort and determination to make discoveries. Discovery leads to joy and rapture. When the excitement of discovery wanes and comfort sets in, this comfort leads to relaxation and tranquility of mind allowing for concentration. Close concentration begets clear awareness and ultimately the student reaches a state of equanimity where reality is accepted without desire or aversion to change. If you followed my rudimentary explanation, the first step is mindfulness; the last step is enlightenment. I'm not suggesting you must become a yogi to practice mindfulness; this was just an outline of formalized principles. If you would like to dive deeper, look into the Four Noble Truths (Dukkha, Samudaya, Nirodha, and Magga which define the Noble Eightfold Path).[57]

Mindfulness as it is contemporarily known and practiced in Western cultures is complicated. In many ways, the practice has been divorced from religion and is a neuroscience tool; however, many describe practicing mindfulness as a spiritual act that elicits a spiritual response. When practicing mindfulness, the individual is focused on the "memory of the present." If you are able to block out the past and not worry about the future for even a few seconds, you interrupt the automatic thoughts that trigger automatic behavior. This suspension of judgment and the ability to consider things in the here and now is what makes mindfulness attractive to leaders and organizations. How often do you think to yourself that your job would be so much easier if you could just clear your mind? If you're being honest with yourself, I would guess the answer is more often than you think.

The above definition of mindfulness traces its roots to Burma (now known as Myanmar). From the late nineteenth century until after World War II, the British controlled Burma as a colony. A largely Buddhist region, the Burmese monks were concerned that colonization would affect how the religion would be viewed by citizens born under British rule. In response, a Burmese monk, Ledi Sayadaw, established a contemporary movement meant to spread insight meditation, or mindful consideration of one's experience, to those outside the monastery. This shift in thinking not only kept Buddhism alive for the nearly sixty years of British occupation but also sparked the notion that everyone could benefit from mindful practices.

While Sayadaw was bringing insight meditation to the people of Burma, Buddhism was being suppressed in Japan during the Meiji Restoration. Born into this period, however, was D.T. Suzuki who would be credited with spreading Buddhism and its principles to wide audiences in Europe and the Americas. Suzuki, a student of Zen Buddhism, was asked to move to the United States and work on translating texts of Eastern religions into English for publication in the West. While Chicago was his home base, Suzuki traveled throughout the US and Europe from the late 1890s until his return to Japan to become a professor in 1909. His influence through speaking engagements and his *Essays in Zen Buddhism* (published during the 1920s and 1930s)[58] introduced mindfulness to new areas of the world.

Suzuki's work set the stage for Buddhism to become a part of the American counterculture. Both the Beats of the 1950s and Hippies of the 1960s borrowed Buddhist tenets such as the rejection of economic materialism and the questioning of traditional values. Famed Beat Poet Gary Snyder wrote of a direct line between Buddhist thought and the counterculture's spirit of social activism. Insight meditation centers began to crop up around the United States where people could go to learn Zen Buddhism. Jon Kabat-Zinn opened the Stress Relief Clinic at UMass Medical School in 1979 with a focus on reducing stress and pain through Mindfulness-Based Stress Reduction (MBSR) and Mindful Cognitive Behavioral Therapy (CBT).[59] Mindfulness was everywhere, which was great. The unfortunate side of this mass appeal has allowed for exploitation in the form of corporate-focused retreats that promise all the wonderful things mindfulness has to offer without the discipline needed to incorporate it into daily life. Therein lies the need for differentiating between the magazines at the grocery store and how mindfulness contributes to Resonant Leadership.

Boyatzis and McKee connected mindfulness to Resonant Leadership by suggesting that leaders can leverage their emotional intelligence to attune their positive feelings to connect with the feelings of others. Those positive vibes then resonate throughout the team to bring about the increased performance studied by Goleman. Practicing and implementing Emotional Intelligence requires self-awareness, self-management, social awareness, and relationship management; all of which have great influence (either positive or negative) over an organization. If the leader displays negative feelings, they are practicing dissonant leadership which leads to people keeping their thoughts and feelings bottled up for fear of ridicule or retribution. Resonant Leadership encourages emotional comfort, cooperation, and the creation of bonds that will help the team stick together in tough times. Engagement begets success, as long as that engagement is positive.

Chapter 17

Quiet Leadership: Rock

"Most people do not listen with the intent to understand; they listen with the intent to reply."
—Stephen Covey

David Rock is a neuroscientist who gained notoriety for his theory of Neuroleadership. His work couples brain research with leadership development, proposing that people can refine their leadership abilities by focusing on four core activities: decision-making and problem-solving, regulating their emotions, collaborating with others, and facilitating change.[60] In addition to founding the NeuroLeadership Institute, which works with numerous Fortune 500 companies on brain and behavior-informed leadership practices, Rock is also a best-selling author. His 2006 book *Quiet Leadership: Six Steps to Transforming Performance at Work* outlines the leadership lesson of the next story.

When practicing Quiet Leadership, the leader allows the

team space to brainstorm and hypothesize solutions. Rather than actively engaging, the leader guides others in the application of their expertise. This is achieved by practicing active listening. The term "active listening" has become a bit of a buzzword in education and business circles; a basic definition I use with medical students who are learning how to interact with patients is "listening to understand and not to respond." Active listening relies heavily on building one's empathy (understanding someone's feelings), sympathy (feeling emotions from someone's experience), and humility (understanding one's limitations). People who practice active listening consistently build in nuances like nonverbal prompts, short verbal affirmations, asking open-ended questions, and paraphrasing to check for understanding, all of which help to gain the trust of their conversation partner.

The active listening skills associated with Quiet Leadership can be difficult as they involve suspending expectations, predictions, and desired outcomes. Our brains naturally want to anticipate where a conversation is going so that we can respond promptly and coherently. The goal of active listening is to pay attention to what is being said so that you can fully understand before formulating a response. Doing so means the leader may be more reserved than expected during interactions with team members.

The *quiet* part of Quiet Leadership ends when the leader is ready to address the team by providing guidance and encouragement. The goal of Quiet Leadership is to provide the most effective feedback based on both the wisdom of the leader and a complete understanding of the situation. The leader is uniquely situated to motivate the team by providing specific, positive feedback on ideas that will bring about the desired change while recommending new courses of action for ideas that still need more consideration. Leaders practicing this model avoid overly emotional responses in times of either crisis or success. Quiet Leadership requires the leader to remain calm, confident, and resilient. It is through an evident passion for the success of the project that the leader keeps the team engaged and feeling valued, not by making fiery or passionate proclamations.

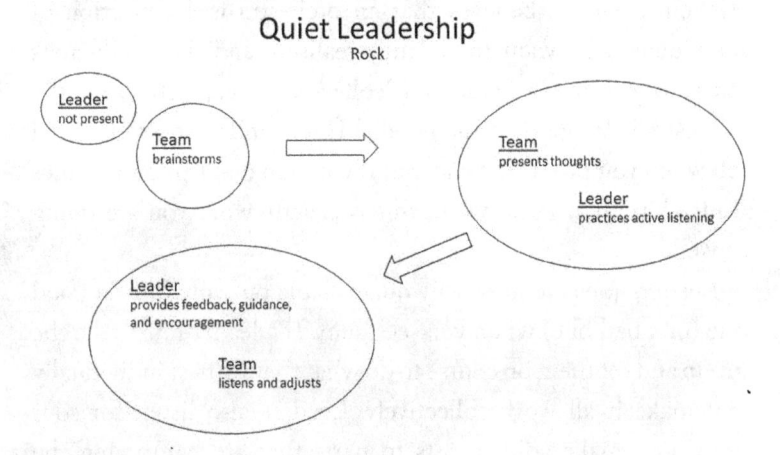

Quiet Leadership
Rock

- Leader not present
- Team brainstorms
- Team presents thoughts
- Leader practices active listening
- Leader provides feedback, guidance, and encouragement
- Team listens and adjusts

The Orchestra and the ER

After class one day, a student named Ara asked if I had ever heard the expression, "The only person in the orchestra without an instrument is the conductor." While I was sure I had, I hadn't considered it in the context to which he was referring. We had been discussing leadership in medicine and how it is often easier to describe what a leader *does* than what a leader *is*. The role isn't always well defined, but someone has to make decisions and that person better be someone with extensive knowledge, critical thinking skills, situational awareness, and, ideally, years of wisdom.

This conversation led me to do some research and I found a BBC article outlining the role of the conductor in an orchestra. In the article, famed conductor Pierre Boulez is quoted as saying, "You have to impose your will—not with a hammer, but you have to be able to convince people of your point of view."[61] The article also shared the thoughts of Tom Service, a broadcaster and journalist who studied conductors for his book Music as Alchemy. Service believes that an orchestra is a collection of individuals who want to be "fully realised" and the conductor's job is to give the individuals a "collective focus;" otherwise, the orchestra is "rudderless and bereft." This sounds like a really hard job when you put it that way, but if your job description includes leadership, then guess what, this is exactly what you are doing as well.

Leaders' jobs are not easily quantifiable but you know a good one (or a bad one) when you see them. The leader must take the group and set them on course to do what they do best individually and make it all work collectively. Leaders also listen for sour notes and make adjustments to parts that are hampering the success of the whole. Leaders act as a conduit from employees to stakeholders in the same way that the conductor is the conduit from the orchestra to the audience. As Boulez puts it, "You have to know the culture, to know the score, and to project what you want to hear."

Within this frame, outcomes tend to be a strange mixture of involvement and disengagement. When successful, the leader gets the glory whether they are comfortable with it or not. If unsuccessful, they get the blame. They might be heavily involved in the decision-making process, which makes the glory or blame justified. Conversely, if they aren't heavily involved in the outcome, they may still get the glory or blame as the figurehead or "name" that people associate with the organization. This can make for an elaborate juggling act and can be tough on the psyche. Jim Collins, author of *Good to Great*, tells us, "Focus on the process, not the outcome."[62] In other words, allow others to focus on outcomes while the leader focuses on process. In the same way world-class conductors developed the skills to immortalize whatever piece they are leading, effective leaders create systems that can be replicated and implemented for further success both inside and outside their organizations.

Ara is a future physician and our conversation made me consider where the conductor analogy applies to medicine. I decided the role of the conductor was analogous to the role of the Team Leader during a trauma primary survey. The primary survey is vital to Emergency Medical Service (EMS) workers and Emergency Room (ER) personnel alike. In the field, EMS are instructed to check D-R-A-B-C. Is there any risk of *danger* (i.e., cars, violence)? Is the patient *responsive*? Is the *airway* clear? Is the patient *breathing*? Does the patient have good *circulation*?

The primary survey is repeated when the patient arrives at the emergency department, and the conductor of that orchestra is the Team Leader. The Team Leader is the physician with the highest level of trauma care skills. They are determined ahead of time and are clearly identifiable, often literally with a red sticker or vest signifying them as the leader. The Team Leader ensures proper preparation for the patient's arrival and a clean handoff from EMS to hospital staff. An ER team may vary but in a trauma setting the following people are usually involved: an airway specialist, doctors other than the Team Leader, nurses, and a scribe. Additional imaging specialists and surgeons are at the ready if necessary.[63]

Like a conductor, the Team Leader takes a hands-off role and coordinates care. They direct resuscitation, make critical decisions, and prioritize care while the rest of the team implements treatment. An effective Team Leader must have strong communication skills and practice situational awareness. You can find the Team Leader at the foot of the bed, not unlike the conductor at the podium, with no instrument in hand but conducting the process.

The idea of being the Team Leader on a primary survey is well documented as a stressful but exciting possibility for medical students. Since I will never be one, I don't feel qualified to write about it. I asked Ara to share a few of his thoughts, below.

> I vividly remember the first time I attended a concert by the Los Angeles Philharmonic Orchestra. To say my musical background is limited would be an understatement—even still, I was mesmerized by how the combination of so many different instruments manifested such harmonious sounds. Additionally, the person overseeing the musical flow was waving an instrument that made no sound at all! As I began working within the medical setting, I wondered if this fascinating dynamic would translate to teams within medicine (and beyond). Certainly, as with most teams, the strength of a medical unit can be largely found in the variety of expertise among the members that make up the unit. This may also present the biggest challenge—how do we ensure that the oboe and cello, two

fundamentally different classes of instruments, complement rather than obstruct one another?

Consider, for example, a critical care environment involving a patient in dire condition: there is a physician at the helm overseeing the patient's status, nurses obtaining samples and slipping in and out of the room with essential equipment or information, a respiratory therapist at the bedside monitoring the patient's breathing capacity, radiology technicians maneuvering large portable imaging modalities to gather more information, a scribe documenting vital information, and so on. So many different instruments! How does this result in any efficient progress? And what is the role of Quiet Leadership in this instance?

Over time, I have come to understand that the role of the leader is not to have the loudest instrument; in fact, it's quite the opposite: the role of the leader is to foster cohesive flow so that he or she should not make any sound at all. Consider a less acute setting: physicians work in both clinical and academic medicine to educate and manage team members—often students—over extended periods to deliver high-quality care and save lives. This isn't achieved with a megaphone, but through protocol, repetition, simulation, and education. There is a shared goal that facilitates accountability among members, often reinforced between them. This can even establish a sense of 'group leadership.'

The role of the physician, then, is to ensure that these necessary systems are in place. Does everybody on board agree with the direction the ship is sailing? Is one instrument too quiet? Another too loud? Once this harmony among members is achieved, there is not much more that needs to be said. In other words, Quiet Leadership is an effect, rather than a cause, of successful teamwork and preparation.

I mention the story of the orchestra to emphasize the distorted view of leadership that I developed throughout my adolescence and early adulthood. Like many others, I had internalized the popular tropes in media that highlight the boisterous qualities or outcomes of leadership—which is what many find most exciting or thrilling—while critically overlooking the apparent ennui of Quiet Leadership, which includes diligent and monotonous preparation and execution. Given that the role of the physician is founded on being a leader, the notion can attract individuals with dangerous perspectives on what it means to be a successful or effective physician. Highlighting the importance of Quiet Leadership, therefore, can lead to the development of more impactful and thoughtful future physician-leaders. —A.K.

Chapter 18

Resilient Leadership: Duggan, Moyer, and Theurer

"Only those who dare to fail greatly, can ever achieve greatly."
— Robert F. Kennedy

Resiliency as a subject of psychological research began with Norman Garmezy's 1985 publication of *Stress-Resistant Children: The Search for Protective Factors*. Garmezy's early career focused on schizophrenia but shifted when he arrived at the Institute of Child Development at the University of Minnesota in 1961. He was interested in determining why some children remained resilient in the face of stress while others succumbed to adjustment issues. Garmezy and subsequent researchers found that resilient children displayed identifiable protective factors. One such factor is the belief that they control their environment and not the converse, known as internal locus of control. Another concerns the child's response to trauma or a

Resilient Leadership
Duggan, Moyer, and Theurer

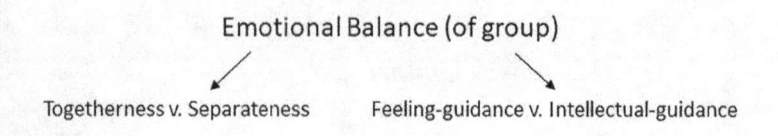

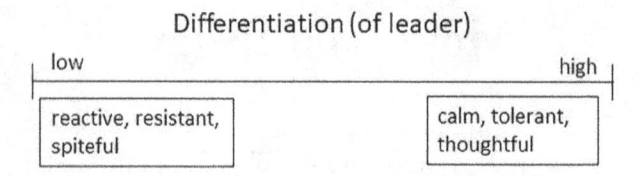

Emotional Balance (of group)

Togetherness v. Separateness Feeling-guidance v. Intellectual-guidance

Differentiation (of leader)

low	high
reactive, resistant, spiteful	calm, tolerant, thoughtful

stressful experience: children who viewed a stressful situation as something to learn from or overcome showed greater success than those who dwelled on the negativity of the experience.[64] Teaching these protective factors became the basis for fostering resilience in children and adults.

One factor connected to resiliency is the ability to stay in the present, a challenge for many of us. The past is over; there's nothing that can be done about it. The future hasn't happened yet, and while our present actions will shape those portions of our future we can control, an infinite number of factors we don't control will ultimately determine the future. The present is the only time when we can feel or achieve anything. Despite this, people pine for "the one that got away" or spend hours awake at night worrying about work the next day. These thoughts aren't helpful and our most deep-seated fears probably aren't going to come to pass, no matter what our 2 a.m. brain tells us.

While not easy to do, quashing doubt and learning from setbacks are two strategies that Garmezy identified for fostering mental resilience. Another resilience strategy identified by Carl Rogers is self-talk, which can be categorized as negative, positive, or neutral.[65]

Negative self-talk is the result of doubt and fear. These are often intrusive thoughts that can have negative effects on mental state and physical performance. To overcome negative self-talk, we can recognize and reframe these thoughts.

Positive self-talk is a set of strategies used to recenter ourselves. It can pull the individual out of an illogical mindset and back to thinking clearly. One example of positive self-talk is reality testing: "I've done this before and I can do it again." Compassionate self-talk asks what is needed from others: "Am I looking for solutions to my problem or just wanting to be seen and heard?" Self-disputing is a strategy in which a negative thought is challenged with logic: "I might think I'm never going to feel better but that's not true. Nothing can last forever, especially not this funk I'm in."

Neutral self-talk is an interesting concept. People who are good at self-regulation can live in neutral. In fact, people who tend to automatically look at things with a negative mindset might be better off living in neutral. When practicing neutral self-talk, the individual identifies a problem, and then their rational mind tells them what needs to happen next. Not getting overly emotional allows the rational mind to take over until the problem is resolved. Like mindfulness, a neutral mind is a mind occupied by the here and now. It's primed to respond as opposed to exhausted by worry.

Resilient Leadership is a term that was coined by Bob

Duggan and Jim Moyer in 2009[66] and expanded upon by their colleague Bridgette Theurer in 2017.[67] The model is based on psychiatrist Murray Bowen's work on Family Systems Theory, as applied to organizations. Bowen believed that negativity spreads through families like a contagion.[68] Since family units depend on one another for support and generally live in the same space, the negative experience of one member affects all members of the group. Negativity from the head(s) of the household is even more destructive as the others look to that person for guidance and leadership.

Bowen encouraged his patients to see that emotional processes dictate the rationality or irrationality of their decisions and that finding emotional balance helps create harmony. One of those balances is *togetherness vs. separateness:* individuals operating in groups must identify and value their sense of self while remaining cognizant of their role within the organization independent of each role. The second structure is *feeling guidance system vs. intellectual guidance system*: the individual must find equilibrium between their feelings and instincts and their logical thinking and reason. Reaching the appropriate conclusion requires both.

Duggan, Moyer, and Theurer believe that once a leader has considered effective resiliency strategies they reach a level of differentiation. Leaders with high differentiation are thoughtful, calm, tolerant of stress, and less reactive. They don't give in to pressure and have an easier time building relationships with followers. Undifferentiated leaders are emotionally reactive and tend to repeat the same mistakes. They give in to the most vocal colleagues while exercising unnecessary pressure on passive colleagues to give themselves a greater sense of control and power.

Differentiated leaders view resilience as an adaptation in the face of adversity, but that adaptation is only effective when the leader responds with the most effective emotional process. The disposition of the leader has the greatest effect on the organization, just like the head(s) of the household in Bowen's example. How the leader presents themselves affects the entire organization, even those with whom they have no direct contact, as all employees feel a connection to the leader.

Duggan, Moyer, and Theurer use the analogy of an iceberg to explain a hidden chemistry that exists in organizations. The rational decisions an organization releases to the public are the visible tip of the iceberg. The emotional regulation of the entire organization required to make those rational decisions is the behemoth beneath the water's surface. The leader's ability to present the appropriate emotional behavior is more important than any individual personality trait. Calm begets calm, anxiety begets anxiety.

Flush it!

If I asked you to name a golfer who has won the PGA Championship Tournament, you would probably say Tiger Woods or Jack Nicklaus, and you would be correct. Both have won the tournament five times. Other notable names like Phil Mickelson, Ben Hogan, and Walter Hagen (the only other five-time winner) make the list. Even the complex yet loveable John Daly made an appearance in the winner's column in 1991. A name unfamiliar to most who don't follow golf closely is the 2013 winner, Jason Dufner. Dufner won with a combined ten under par which is a better score than more high-profile recent winners like Brooks Koepka and Justin Thomas. But we're not here to talk about them. August 11, 2013, was "Duf's" day.

Jason Dufner entered the 2013 PGA Championship at forty-to-one odds. At the end of the first round (the PGA Championship is four rounds in total), Dufner, the twenty-first-ranked golfer in the world, was tied for sixth at two under par. Not bad. He was setting himself up for a pretty nice payday. Instead, he made a run for first place. Duf shot a course-record seven under par in Round Two which included an eagle and took the lead by two strokes. The third round, however, was a different story. While Dufner shot a respectable seventy-one, he was caught for the lead by veteran Jim Furyk. Dufner would have to make a comeback in the final round if he was going to win his first major championship.

Oddly enough, this was not an unfamiliar place for Jason Dufner. At the same event in 2011, he was tied for first place after the second round and sat alone atop the leaderboard after the third. But in a disastrous end to the final round, Dufner bogeyed three of the last four holes giving away the lead and the championship to Keegan Bradley. On the night before the final round in 2013, perhaps Dufner had that "here we go again" feeling. Would he come up short again for the second time in three years?

From a standpoint of resilience, Dufner had two options. Option 1: Dwell on the fact that he just lost the lead before the final round, remember that he lost the lead at the end of the final round in 2011, and let those negative thoughts affect his performance. Option 2: Flush any negative thoughts! While not easy to do, Dufner could remain calm, objectively look at the situation, and try a few resilience-boosting strategies such as the following:

> *Reality testing.* "I set the record on Friday with seven under. All I need is two under on Sunday and I have a shot."
>
> *Self-disputing.* "What happened two years ago has nothing to do with what is going to happen tomorrow. They are two completely separate events and I'm a different person now than I was then."
>
> *Compassionate self-talk.* "Either talk to a coach, analyzing my swing to figure out what to improve, or take a deep breath, unwind, and talk through what I'm feeling with a loved one."

While I don't know what Dufner did to get ready for the final round, I do know he won the tournament that Sunday, the eleventh of August.

In the chapter on Resonant Leadership, I said that leaders can act as an "emotional contagion." When faced with adversity, colleagues look to leadership for guidance and, perhaps more importantly, a steady hand. Leaders who practice resilience have learned to remain composed during stressful times, which limits anxiety and diffuses tension within the group.

Helpful self-talk for the leader is no different from anyone else. Resilient leaders keep the situation in perspective and try not to blow it out of proportion while still preparing for unexpected developments. Stressful situations tend to be ambiguous and uncertain; however, even if you lost the lead on Saturday, remaining flexible and calm are the best ways to win on Sunday.

Chapter 19

Vulnerable Leadership: Morgan

> "People sometimes got the wrong impression of Thurman, that he was grumpy, that he was a tough guy. He wasn't like that at all. To me he was friendly, witty, charming, a real good friend."
> —Lou Piniella, talking about Thurman Munson

Showing vulnerability as a leader may seem contradictory to the last chapter on resilience. These two concepts provide further proof that organizations and people are complex and the ability to respond most appropriately is more valuable than a singular leadership style. Furthermore, resilience and vulnerability aren't as different as you might think.

The emotions of leadership have been studied extensively. As noted earlier, *encourage the heart* is not only one of Kouzes and Posner's practices of exemplary leadership but the one they say is most important. Robert Greenleaf popularized the notion of Servant Leadership throughout the 1960s and '70s.

This philosophy suggested that power is a privilege given to the leader and it should be exercised exclusively to meet the needs of everyone in the organization. If the leader is focused on providing followers with what they need to succeed, then progress and growth become natural occurrences.[69]

In the 2023 book *Leading with Vulnerability*, Jacob Morgan presented the distinct difference between being vulnerable and practicing Vulnerable Leadership. For example, just admitting a mistake may leave a leader vulnerable, but admitting a mistake and sharing what they learned portrays the leader as a regular person who grows from their mistakes. Another example is talking about personal challenges or struggles. While this can be a good way for leaders to connect with others and build trust, it should not be a therapy session. Leaders must consider who they are sharing with, when is the best time to share, and the correct tone to use, and they should focus on framing the personal struggle as an illustration of professional growth.

Practicing Vulnerable Leadership can provide huge benefits but it can also be difficult. Morgan surveyed leaders and asked why they weren't comfortable being vulnerable around their colleagues. The most common answers were that they didn't want to appear weak or incompetent, the culture doesn't encourage admitting when you're wrong, and they feared rejection, dismissal, or that an admission would be used against them. These fears create a leadership culture where it is more beneficial to pretend everything is fine than to admit we are humans who make mistakes.

Morgan presented Eight Attributes of Vulnerable Leaders[70] to combat the perception that you have to be perfect if you are in charge.

Self-awareness: How do the leader's actions affect those around them?
Self-compassion: How do leaders find ways to be kind to themselves?
Self-confidence: How does the leader display a belief in self with a vision for growth and success?
Empathy: What is the best way to consider things from others' perspectives?
Authenticity: How does the leader present themselves as their genuine self?
Integrity: How does the leader present their vision with an honest and clear set of values?
Competence: What does success look like and how can the leader deliver it?
Motivation: How does the leader inspire others to take action and improve?

Vulnerable Leadership
Morgan

Self-awareness	How do your actions affect others?
Self-compassion	How are you kind to yourself?
Self-confidence	How do you display a vision for your success and growth?
Empathy	How do you consider other's perspectives?
Authenticity	How do you present as your genuine self?
Integrity	How do you present a clear set of values?
Competence	How do you define and deliver success?
Motivation	How do you inspire others to improve?

Part 1: The Magic Shop

Jim was what you might call a *free-range kid*. He spent most of the summer of 1968 (the summer before he started eighth grade) riding his bike around the wind-swept desert city of Lancaster, California, with pretty much no supervision. He wasn't looking forward to going back to school because he didn't particularly like it, but he didn't want to be home either. His father drank too much and his mother slept most of the day to cope with her husband's behavior. Jim worried about his parents and his brother who was often bullied. He often felt aimless and struggled to control his outbursts which led to trouble. But one thing Jim really enjoyed was magic. He was quite good at the sleight of hand tricks. His friends marveled as he made cigarettes appear from thin air. One day, Jim rode his bike to an unfamiliar part of town. He came upon a strip mall and was stopped in his tracks by the sign above one of the shops, "Cactus Rabbit Magic Shop." Jim was a little apprehensive. He loved magic but wasn't very good at talking to people. He didn't smile much on account of having a brown front tooth, the result of an accident that his parents didn't have money to pay a dentist to fix. Jim timidly entered the shop and was greeted by a friendly woman behind the counter. Her name was Ruth and she was the owner's mother. Ruth took a liking to Jim and offered to teach him some *real magic*. Jim was apprehensive but figured he had nothing better to do so he agreed. Ruth had two conditions. The first was that Jim was to come back every day for six weeks as that was as long as Ruth was staying in California. The second was that Jim had to teach the magic to someone else.

For the agreed-upon six weeks, Jim and Ruth worked on skills like relaxing the body, controlled breathing, controlled internal monologue, and visualization. The magic was working. Jim didn't feel so lost or angry anymore. His problems weren't magically solved, but he felt much more in control of his circumstances.

Jim was sad when Ruth left but he knew she wasn't staying long.

Jim remembered the lessons Ruth taught him as he grew older. He had an interest in medicine but didn't have the best grades and wasn't sure how to go about getting into college. A friend told him they were applying to the University of California at Irvine and asked where he was considering. Not knowing what to say, Jim said he was also considering Irvine. He applied and was a bit surprised when he was accepted.

As Jim's confidence grew, he decided to pursue medical school, although his 2.53 GPA was not very impressive to his professors. So much so that the department secretary denied him a meeting to discuss a recommendation for his medical school application, claiming, "It would be a waste of everyone's time." Jim insisted on talking to the recommendation committee and, when he eventually got the opportunity, passionately described how a doctor is not a number. He secured a recommendation from his UC-Irvine professors and through remediation was accepted to one medical school (Tulane University) where he excelled.

Jim became Dr. James Doty. He worked as an Army surgeon and later went into practice as a neurosurgeon and entrepreneur. Through hard work and wise investments, Doty's wealth grew. He did not forget the people who gave him a shot when others denied him. After Hurricane Katrina ravaged New Orleans, Doty donated enough money to endow the dean's position and rebuild the library at Tulane, further proof that a snapshot in time cannot predict a person's success. He never forgot the lessons that Ruth taught him, and in medical school he learned about the magic of neuroplasticity, Cognitive Behavioral Therapy, and the sympathetic nervous system. Ruth taught Jim that changing his worldview could change the circumstances around him. CBT works by helping people change maladaptive thinking patterns. Twelve-year-old Jim viewed himself as "bad" and as such wasn't surprised when bad things happened. If we can change our view of ourselves, we can more clearly make decisions that change unwanted behaviors.

Dr. Doty outlines his journey which spans much more than I shared above in his amazing memoir, *Into the Magic Shop: A Neurosurgeon's Quest to Discover the Mysteries of the Brain and the Secrets of the Heart*,[71] and shares what he learned along the way as the founder of the Center for Compassion and Altruism Research and Education at Stanford University.

Pretty great story, huh? But what does this have to do with vulnerable leadership? I was in the audience when Dr. Doty spoke at the Association of American Medical Colleges conference in 2019. At one point during his presentation, he choked up and began to cry. He acknowledged getting emotional but appeared to make it a point not to apologize. If you watch any of Dr. Doty's presentations, chances are he will pause, choke up, and maybe even shed a tear. He is the only presenter I have ever seen who gets so openly emotional during his presentations. Keep in mind, he is a surgeon who was trained that emotions are the enemy and an admitted former juvenile delinquent who spent a lot of his childhood acting like a tough guy when in actuality he was operating in survival mode. In one interview, Doty mentions being approached by a psychiatrist after a speaking engagement. The woman said she felt so bad for him and hoped that he wasn't too embarrassed. She offered to help him get over the perceived weakness of crying in front of a room full of people. What the psychiatrist didn't understand is that people who can show emotion are often the strongest people in the room, because they aren't afraid to be genuine and authentic about their passions. People shed tears of joy but sometimes tears are representations of appreciation, tenacity, pride, or gratitude. These *happy tears* (as my seven-year-old son calls them) often replace anguish, pain, and sadness as the person remembers how they shook off negative emotions and moved forward, damaged perhaps but certainly stronger. Vulnerable leaders have earned those tears and don't shy away from emotions that can inspire greatness in themselves and others around them.

Part 2: Some Old Cardboard
Thurman Munson was the captain of the New York Yankees starting in 1976, the team's first since Lou Gehrig. A fan favorite, Munson was a seven-time all-star who played eleven years with the Yankees. His life ended tragically in a plane crash at the age of thirty-two. With all due respect to Thurman Munson's memory, he is a minor character in this story.

One of my passions is baseball cards. I used to get in trouble as a kid because my allowance (and then some) went to the local card shop almost immediately after it was in my hands. I stopped collecting in high school but got back into the hobby in my early thirties. My collection has a few nice high-end cards but a large portion of our basement is boxes of cards hardly worth the paper they are printed on. My wife asked me one day if I had any Thurman Munson cards. I responded with a perplexed, "Probably. Why?" She tolerates my collecting obsession but never really had much interest beyond enjoying my childlike excitement when I acquired a sought-after card. She explained that a friend's husband, Dean, had cancer and wasn't doing well. Dean had sold his prized baseball card collection in the late

1970s to buy his wife an engagement ring. Thurman Munson was his favorite player, so she wanted to buy a Munson card from me to give to him.

While Munson was a great player, I explained that his stuff didn't sell for big bucks beyond a high-grade rookie card. I dug through my boxes and came up with a few soft-cornered and sun-bleached Munsons and she gave them to her for Dean. A few days later, her friend reported that the cards brightened his day and she saw him get excited for the first time in a long time. So I did what anyone would do. I asked for their address, and I dug up every Thurman Munson and older Yankee I could find (admittedly, as a Mets fan, these weren't hard for me to part with). Every week or so, I mailed Dean a couple of cards, sometimes including a letter wishing him well. Eventually, I sent a binder for him to keep the cards in. He expressed appreciation through his wife—he was unable to write back—and it made me feel good to be able to cheer up someone who was going through such a struggle.

When Dean died, I felt like a friend had passed, even though we had never met in person nor talked on the phone. I was sad but we had known this was the more than likely outcome. His wife continued to say that receiving the baseball cards was something he looked forward to and enjoyed.

This story was always something I was proud of, but I never got too emotional about the experience until one day when my students and I were discussing their community immersion projects. For this project, a pair of students work with a community partner, usually someone who is living with a chronic illness or an elderly person. The discussion turned to end-of-life and my mind turned to Dean and the Yankees cards.

I had also recently suffered the loss of my dad, who passed away from Lewy body dementia in 2017. I had witnessed his decline over five years, with the last months being horrible. I knew he would not have wanted to live that way, and the stress took a huge toll on my mom, despite her background as a nurse and me helping as best I could. When my cousin hugged me at the funeral, crying on my shoulder, I had to explain to him that this was better. He looked at me with a bit of disbelief.

The end-of-life discussion in class that day came about when one of my students said that she and her partner were working with a couple in their eighties who were relatively self-sufficient but their health problems were catching up to them. We talked about the importance of a support system and how the couple would rely on each other until one of them was gone. They had grown children in the area who were able to help with their parents so that was a positive. I told my students the story of Dean. It's the only time (so far) I couldn't hold back tears in class, and we often talk about heavy stuff. I initially tried to swallow the lump in my throat. When that didn't work, I tried to laugh it off. But when my voice cracked, there was no holding back. Considering the interaction now, I'm glad I had to take a moment to let it out. It wasn't a therapy session; it was a learning moment for my students that built trust and strengthened our bond. They not only saw their professor as a human being with real emotions, but they were also reminded that practicing patient-centered medicine involves being vulnerable.

Conclusion

Lakeside

I am writing this sitting on the screened-in porch at our family cabin on Dog Pond (look it up on a map—it really does look like a dog from overhead). My wife and our youngest are pushing off from the dock in their kayak with my mother-in-law in tow. They are delivering socks and baby supplies that our son has outgrown to some friends across the lake.

While I would probably sell more books if I told you I utilized the principles outlined in these pages to make a million dollars and buy this lakefront property in a New England paradise, I would be lying. My father-in-law purchased the "camp" thirty years ago and remodeled the cabin into a beautiful home that can be lived in most of the year (see: Vermont winters; New England mud season). My wife has been coming here since she was a little girl. I didn't realize it at the time but my first invitation here a few years ago was a tentative "welcome to the family." Today, we just attended our first lake meeting with her parents. Everyone was very friendly, and let's not kid ourselves, obviously well-off. I discussed liberal arts colleges, loon conservation, and a fellow academic doctor's eighteen months living in Alaska monitoring water quality. It's been a beautiful weekend and the significance of a generation transitioning its treasure (both physical and figurative) to the next is not lost on me.

Sitting on this porch listening to the water hit the shore and

Conclusion

feeling the breeze through the pine trees clears my mind. It reminds me that sometimes things happen only when we are ready for them to occur, on their own timeline. I came here with no plan to write. My goals were to make the eight-hour drive, unplug from work for three days which is something I admittedly struggle to do, and drive home on Tuesday. Then, on a solitary morning drive back to the cabin from our favorite coffee shop, my brain clicked that this was an opportunity to write the conclusion for this leadership journey. I borrowed a notebook from Katie's bag and started scribbling.

Had I said to myself that I was going to write the conclusion while at the lake, I may not have been able to do it, or it might have felt forced, and it certainly wouldn't have been this story. When you choose a profession and devote your life to it, it is nearly impossible to turn it off and you probably wouldn't want to if you could. Your instinct becomes to seek out your passion everywhere you look. This is why medical doctors seem to always be on guard and teachers can't help but look out for children. The positive, however, is that you see the thing you are so committed to all around you. A man at the lake meeting this afternoon took pride in being the association president even as he begged someone else to do it next year. The small business owners fuel the economies of their hometowns even if many of the dollars come from the out-of-town loon conservation set like us.

Sometimes leadership is conflicting and messy (and sometimes it bites). The two years of research that went into this handbook provided me with a twisting and turning sense of how leadership theory has evolved from a search for definitions and traits to seeking an understanding of reactions and emotions. Sometimes leadership is what you do day to day. Sometimes it's jotting down ideas while you attempt to unplug in nature's splendor (I technically did unplug, as this was written by hand with no internet assistance). Noticing the sparks of inspiration within you and radiating from the others around you can help you appreciate the progress we all make in recognizing our potential.

I genuinely hope you enjoyed reading this book and I hope you have taken some bites that will help your leadership life bite less. Feel free to share any of the stories here to help others along their journeys. My parting wisdom is something my mom always says: "Everything in its season." As I mentioned in the introduction, this book found me and was only ready to be written once I sufficiently understood leadership and effective storytelling. Perhaps it's now my season, a full eighteen years into my profession. Continue to learn. Continue to grow. Don't jump at every opportunity simply because it has presented itself. Do what's right for you and only when you are ready.

Endnotes

1 Carmine Gallo, The Storyteller's Secret: From TED Speakers to Business Legends: Why Some Ideas Catch On and Others Don't (New York: St. Martin's Press, 2016).

2 Daniel Goleman, A Force for Good: The Dalai Lama's Vision for Our World (New York: Bloomsbury, 2015).

3 M. H. Abrams and Geoffrey Harpham, A Glossary of Literary Terms, 11th ed. (Boston: Cengage, 2015).

4 Bert Alan Spector, "Carlyle, Freud, and the Great Man Theory More Fully Considered," Leadership 12, no. 2 (2015): 250– 260.

5 Gordon Allport, Personality: A Psychological Interpretation (New York: Holt, Rinehart, & Winston, 1937).

6 Kurt K. Lewin and Ronald Lippitt, "An Experimental Approach to the Study of Autocracy and Democracy: A Preliminary Note," Sociometry 1, (1938): 292– 300.

7 Adrian Horton, "'They All Got On as One Family': The Story of a Woman Who Lived with Chimps," Guardian, April 29, 2021, https://www.theguardian.com/film/2021/apr/29/lucy-the-human-chimp-hbo-max-documentary.

8 Watson, J. B. (1913). "Psychology as the behaviorist views it." Psychological Review, 20(2), 158–177. https://doi.org/10.1037/h0074428.

9 William M. Baum, Understanding Behaviorism: Behavior, Culture, and Evolution, 3rd ed. (Hoboken, NJ: Wiley-Blackwell, 2017).

10 Robert Tannenbaum and Warren Schmidt, "How to Choose a Leadership Pattern," Harvard Business Review 36, (1958): 95–101.

11 David Pearson and Margaret Gallagher, "The Instruction of Reading Comprehension," Contemporary Educational Psychology 8, no. 3 (1983): 317–344.

12 Lev Vygotsky, Mind in Society: The Development of Higher Psychological Processes (Cambridge: Harvard University Press, 1978).

13 Henry Adams, Tom and Jack: The Intertwined Lives of Thomas Hart Benton and Jackson Pollock (New York: Bloomsbury, 2009).

14 John French and Bertram Raven, "The Bases of Social Power," in Studies in Social Power, ed. Dorwin Cartwright (Ann Arbor: Research Center for Group Dynamics, 1959), 150–167.

15 Rensis Likert, New Patterns of Management (New York: McGraw Hill, 1961).

16 Ralph Stogdill, "Personal Factors Associated with Leadership: A Survey of the Literature," Journal of Psychology 25, (1948): 35–71.

17 Andrew Halpin, "The Behavior of Leaders," Educational Leadership 14, no. 3, (1956): 172– 186.

18 Greg Emmanuel, The 100-Yard War: Inside the 100-Year-Old Michigan-Ohio State Football Rivalry (Trade Paper Press, 2005).

19 Danberg, Tyler. "Woody versus Bo: 'Because I Couldn't Go for Three.'" The Lantern, November 26, 2021. https://www.thelantern.com/2021/11/woody-versus-bo-because-i-couldnt-go-for-three/.

20 Abraham Maslow, "A Theory of Human Motivation," Psychological Review 50, no. 4 (1943): 370–396.

21 Douglas McGregor, The Human Side of Enterprise (New York: McGraw Hill, 1960).

22 William Ouchi, Theory Z: How American Business Can Meet the Japanese Challenge (New York: Basic Books, 1981).

23 Roland Li, "Stanford Professor Says 5-Day Office Week Is Dead. But What's Replacing It?" San Francisco Chronicle, October 17, 2023, https://www.sfchronicle.com/projects//remote-work-survey.

24 Nicholas Bloom, "The Five-Day Office Week Is Dead," New York Times, October 16, 2023, https://www.nytimes.com/2023/10/16/opinion/office-work-home-remote.html.

25 Fred Fiedler, "A Contingency Model of Leadership Effectiveness," Advances in Experimental Social Psychology 1, (1964): 149–190.

26 Alexi Pappas, Bravey: Chasing Dreams, Befriending Pain, and Other Big Ideas (New York: The Dial Press, 2021).

27 Bruce Tuckman, "Development Sequence in Small Groups," Psychological Bulletin 63, no. 6, (1965): 384–399.

28 Bruce Tuckman and Mary Ann Jensen, "Stages of Small-Group Development Revisited," Group and Organization Management 2, no. 4 (1977): 419–427.

29 Farnam Street, "The 'Circle of Competence' Theory Will Help You Make Vastly Smarter Decisions," Business Insider, December 5, 2013, https://www.businessinsider.com/the-circle-of-competence-theory-2013-12.

30 Justin Kruger and David Dunning, "Unskilled and Unaware of It: How Difficulties in Recognizing One's Own Incompetence Lead to Inflated Self-Assessments, Journal of Personality and Social Psychology 77, no. 6 (1999): 1121–1134.

31 Ted Williams and John Underwood, The Science of Hitting (New York: Simon & Schuster, 1986).

32 Ralph Birdsall, The Story of Cooperstown (Fili-Quarian Classics, 2010).

33 Leigh Van Valen, "A New Evolutionary Law," Evolutionary Theory 1, (1973): 1–30.

34 George Miller, "The Magical Number Seven Plus or Minus Two: Some Limits on Our Capacity for Processing Information," Psychological Review 63, no. 2, (1956): 81–97.

35 William Chase and Herbert Simon, "Perception in Chess," Cognitive Psychology 4, no. 1 (1973): 55–81.

36 John Sweller, "Cognitive Load During Problem Solving: Effects on Learning," Cognitive Science 12, no. 2 (1988): 257–285.

37 Freiberger, Marianne. "The Story of the Gömböc." Plus Maths, September 1, 1970. https://plus.maths.org/content/story-gomboc.

38 Nedra Glover Tawwab, Set Boundaries, Find Peace: A Guide to Reclaiming Yourself (New York: Tarcher Perigee, 2021).

39 Marc Knowles and Sookyung Suh, "Performance System Analysis: Learning by Doing," Performance Improvement 44, no. 4 (2005): 35–42.

40 Office of Student Support, "The Eisenhower Matrix," Columbia University School of Professional Studies, August 2023, https://sps.columbia.edu/sites/default/files/2023-08/Eisenhower%20Matrix.pdf.

41 Paul Hersey, Kenneth Blanchard, and Dewey Johnson, Management of Organizational Behavior: Leading Human Resources, 10th ed. (London: Pearson, 2012).

42 Lee Bolman and Terrence Deal, Reframing Organizations: Artistry, Choice, and Leadership, 7th ed. (San Francisco: Jossey-Bass, 2021).

43 Abraham Kaplan, The Conduct of Inquiry: Methodology for Behavioral Science (New York: Routledge, 1973).

44 Abraham Maslow, Psychology of Science: A Reconnaissance (Gateway Editions, 1969).

45 "Hardwick History," Hardwick, VT Historical Society, October 17, 2023, https://hardwickvthistory.org/about-hardwick/hardwick-history/.

46 Bernard Bass, Leadership and Performance Beyond Expectations (New York: Free

Press, 1985).

47 David Cooperrider, "Appreciative Inquiry: Toward a Methodology for Understanding and Enhancing Organizational Innovation" (doctoral dissertation, Case Western Reserve University, 1986), Proquest Dissertations Publishing (Publication No. 8611485).

48 Spencer Johnson, Who Moved My Cheese? (London: Vermillion, 1999).

49 James Kouzes and Barry Posner, The Leadership Challenge: How to Make Extraordinary Things Happen in Organizations, 7th ed. (San Francisco: Jossey-Bass, 2023).

50 Ronald Heifetz, Leadership Without Easy Answers (Cambridge: Harvard University Press, 1998).

51 Ronald Heifetz, Marty Linsky, and Alexander Grashow, The Practice of Adaptive Leadership: Tools and Tactics for Changing Your Organization and the World (Cambridge: Harvard Business Press, 2009).

52 Scott Edinger, "Good Leaders Know You Can't Fight Reality," Harvard Business Review, October 8, 2021, https://hbr.org/2021/10/good-leaders-know-you-cant-fight-reality.

53 https://www.jsonline.com/story/sports/nba/bucks/2023/05/03/bucks-giannis-antetokounmpo-quote-on-failure-after-nba-playoff-loss-sports-world-reacts/70180123007/

54 Malcolm Gladwell, David and Goliath: Underdogs, Misfits, and the Art of Battling Giants (London: Penguin Books, 2014).

55 Daniel Goleman, Emotional Intelligence: Why It Can Matter More Than IQ (New York: Random House, 2005).

56 Richard Boyatzis and Annie McKee, Resonant Leadership: Renewing Yourself and Connecting with Others through Mindfulness, Hope, and Compassion (Cambridge: Harvard Business Review Press, 2005).

57 Devean Chase, Modern Buddhism: Buddha's Ancient Teachings for the Modern Person (independent pub, 2021).

58 Daisetz Teitaro Suzuki, Essays in Zen Buddhism (Third Series), (New York: Samuel Weiser, 1934).

59 Jon Kabat-Zinn, Mindfulness for Beginners: Reclaiming the Present Moment—and Your Life (Louisville, CO: Sounds True, 2016).

60 David Rock and Al Ringleb, Handbook of Neuroleadership (independent pub, 2013).

61 Clemency Burton-Hill, "What Does a Conductor Actually Do?," BBC Culture, October 31, 2014, https://www.bbc.com/culture/article/20141029-what-do-conductors-

actually-do.

62 James Collins, Good to Great: Why Some Companies Make the Leap . . .and Others Don't (New York: Harper Business, 2001).

63 Elizabeth Rosenman, Jeremy Branzetti, and Rosemarie Fernandez, "Assessing Team Leadership in Emergency Medicine: The Milestones and Beyond," Journal of Graduate Medical Education 8, no. 3 (2016): 332–340.

64 Norman Garmezy, Stress Resistant Children: The Search for Protective Factors (Oxford: Oxford Press, 1985)

65 Carl Rogers, "A Theory of Therapy, Personality Relationships as Developed in the Client-Centered Framework" in Psychology: A Study of a Science, ed. Sigmund Koch (New York: McGraw Hill, 1959).

66 Bob Duggan and Jim Moyer, Resilient Leadership: Navigating the Hidden Chemistry of Organizations (independent pub, 2009).

67 Bob Duggan and Bridget Theurer, Resilient Leadership 2.0: Leading with Calm, Clarity, and Conviction in Anxious Times (independent pub, 2017).

68 Murray Bowen, Family Therapy in Clinical Practice (Lanham, MD: Jason Aronson, 1993).

69 Robert Greenleaf, The Power of Servant Leadership (Oakland: Berrett-Koehler, 1998).

70 Jacob Morgan, Leading with Vulnerability: Unlock Your Greatest Superpower to Transform Yourself, Your Team, and Your Organization (Hoboken, NJ: Wiley, 2023).

71 James Doty, Into the Magic Shop: A Neurosurgeon's Quest to Discover the Mysteries of the Brain and the Secrets of the Heart (New York: Avery, 2017).

Acknowledgments

On the journey to bring this project to life, numerous individuals contributed their support and guidance. To those whom I may unintentionally overlook, I offer my sincere apologies.

Jane Warren, your editorial insight was invaluable. You met me where I was, balancing honesty with encouragement, shaping mere words into captivating stories. Without your guidance, this project wouldn't have reached its potential.

Everyone at Rootstock Publishing. I brought this project to you because you felt like a family I wanted to be a part of. Thank you for welcoming me with open arms. A special thanks to publisher Samantha Kolber, editor Amabel Kylee Síorghlas, the designers, layout people, and everyone else who brings the wonderful Rootstock books to life.

My gratitude extends to my students, both those acknowledged within these pages and those who have taught me more than I can give in return. Ara Khoylyan and Haydn Swackhamer, your contributions enriched this book immeasurably. A conversation about the Red Queen Problem with Bennett Stahl reignited the "Cognitive Load" section I was about to abandon. A special mention to Ceili Hamill (the thoughtful future physician in "Learning Leaves, Story Stays") and the remarkable individuals comprising the "best CBL group ever" (Devi, Garrett, Lynzi, Tyler, Yousef, McKinley, and Deven) — your impact transcends

Acknowledgments

these pages, and I anticipate shedding tears of pride at your graduation. Jordan Salvato, your choice to be my research mentee continues to humble and inspire me. Thank you for reminding me that we are our stories.

Thank you to my colleagues, past and present. To my foul fiend Jessica, thanks for always encouraging me to write and I'm sorry I don't call as often as I promised I would. Jim Becker, you showed me how to lead an organization without losing the community you serve. It's easy to be a boss, but it's more important to be yourself. Andrea DiMattia, you encouraged me every step of the way. I always say that coming to GCSOM was my "mid-career" crisis. That leap of faith has turned out to be one of the best decisions I have ever made. Last but certainly not least, thank you to Dr. Robert Gates ("Call me Bob"). My dad was a carpenter and never really "got me" hence why I can barely hang a shelf. I navigated much of my college career flying blind with no real idea of what would define success at the end of the road. Thank you, Bob, for helping me navigate the waters of graduate school, academic life, and publishing while instilling a few life lessons along the way.

To my mother, my steadfast beacon through life's ebbs and flows, I am eternally grateful. To my children, each a source of immeasurable pride in their unique ways, thank you for your patience as I learned how to be a dad. And to my wife Katie, your unwavering support while juggling your own professional ambitions affirmed that ours is a journey shared, now and always.

The countless nights spent typing away, long after my world had fallen asleep, were all justified in holding a physical copy of this book. To everyone who played a role in bringing this work to fruition, I extend my heartfelt thanks. Whether this book reaches a million or ten readers, my pride remains unwavering. This achievement is a testament to the collective effort of so many people beyond myself, and for that, I am profoundly grateful.

About the Author

Dr. McCoog is an assistant Professor at Geisinger Commonwealth School of Medicine in Scranton, Pennsylvania. He studied history, philosophy, and education at Bloomsburg University and earned a doctorate in educational leadership from Wilkes University. Dr. McCoog has published numerous journal articles and began writing creative works after studying narrative-based medicine at the University of Toronto. He was a teacher and school administrator for thirteen years before transitioning to higher education. He was a nominee for the Raise the Line Outstanding Faculty Award and a nominee for best poster International Association of Medical Science Educators.

Ian and his family live in the Susquehanna River Valley of Pennsylvania and enjoy spending the summer months in central Vermont at their cabin on Dog Pond. Visit his website, www.ianmccoog.com.

Bibliography

Abrams, M. H., and Geoffrey Harpham. *A Glossary of Literary Terms*. 11th ed. Boston: Cengage, 2015.

Adams, Henry. *Tom and Jack: The Intertwined Lives of Thomas Hart Benton and Jackson Pollock*. New York: Bloomsbury, 2009.

Allport, Gordon. *Personality: A Psychological Interpretation*. New York: Holt, Rinehart, & Winston, 1937.

Bass, Bernard. *Leadership and Performance Beyond Expectations*. New York: Free Press, 1985.

Baum, William. *Understanding Behaviorism: Behavior, Culture, and Evolution*. 3rd ed. Hoboken, NJ: Wiley-Blackwell, 2017.

Birdsall, Ralph. *The Story of Cooperstown*. Fili-Quarian Classics, 2010.

Bloom, Nicholas. "The Five-Day Office Week Is Dead." New York Times, October 16, 2023. https://www.nytimes.com/2023/10/16/opinion/officeworkhomeremote.html.

Bolman, Lee, and Terrence Deal. *Reframing Organizations: Artistry, Choice, and Leadership*. 7th ed. San Francisco: Jossey-Bass, 2021.

Bowen, Murray. *Family Therapy in Clinical Practice*. Lanham, MD: Jason Aronson, 1993.

Boyatzis, Richard, and Annie McKee. *Resonant Leadership: Renewing Yourself and Connecting with Others through Mindfulness, Hope, and Compassion*. Cambridge: Harvard Business Review Press, 2005.

Burton-Hill, Clemency. "What Does a Conductor Actually Do?" BBC Culture, October 31, 2014. https://www.bbc.com/culture/article/20141029whatdoconductorsactuallydo.

Chase, Devean. *Modern Buddhism: Buddha's Ancient Teachings for the Modern Person*. Independent Publisher, 2021.

Chase, William, and Herbert Simon. "Perception in Chess." *Cognitive Psychology* 4, no. 1 (1973): 55–81.

Collins, James. *Good to Great: Why Some Companies Make the Leap . . . and Others Don't*.

New York: Harper Business, 2001.

Cooperrider, David. "Appreciative Inquiry: Toward a Methodology for Understanding and Enhancing Organizational Innovation." Doctoral dissertation, Case Western Reserve University, 1986. *Proquest Dissertations Publishing* (Publication No. 8611485).

Doty, James. *Into the Magic Shop: A Neurosurgeon's Quest to Discover the Mysteries of the Brain and the Secrets of the Heart*. New York: Avery, 2017.

Duggan, Bob, and Jim Moyer. *Resilient Leadership: Navigating the Hidden Chemistry of Organizations*. Independent Publisher, 2009.

Duggan, Bob, and Bridget Theurer. *Resilient Leadership 2.0: Leading with Calm, Clarity, and Conviction in Anxious Times*. Independent Publisher, 2017.

Edinger, Scott. "Good Leaders Know You Can't Fight Reality." Harvard Business Review, October 8, 2021. https://hbr.org/2021/10/goodleadersknowyoucantfightreality.

Emmanuel, Greg. *The 100-Yard War: Inside the 100-Year-Old Michigan-Ohio State Football Rivalry*. Trade Paper Press, 2005.

Farnam Street (blog). "The 'Circle of Competence' Theory Will Help You Make Vastly Smarter Decisions." Business Insider, December 5, 2013. https://www.businessinsider.com/the-circle-of-competence-theory-2013-12.

Fiedler, Fred. "A Contingency Model of Leadership Effectiveness." *Advances in Experimental Social Psychology* 1 (1964): 149–190.

French, John, and Bertram Raven. "The Bases of Social Power." In *Studies in Social Power*, edited by Dorwin Cartwright, 150–167. Ann Arbor: Research Center for Group Dynamics, 1959.

Gallo, Carmine. *The Storyteller's Secret: From TED Speakers to Business Legends: Why Some Ideas Catch On and Others Don't*. New York: St. Martin's Press, 2016.

Garmezy, Norman. *Stress Resistant Children: The Search for Protective Factors*. Oxford: Oxford University Press, 1985.

Gladwell, Malcolm. *David and Goliath: Underdogs, Misfits, and the Art of Battling Giants*. London: Penguin Books, 2014.

Goleman, Daniel. *Emotional Intelligence: Why It Can Matter More Than IQ*. New York: Random House, 2005.

Goleman, Daniel. *A Force for Good: The Dalai Lama's Vision for Our World*. New York: Bloomsbury, 2015.

Greenleaf, Robert. *The Power of Servant Leadership*. Oakland: Berrett-Koehler, 1998.

Halpin, Andrew. "The Behavior of Leaders." *Educational Leadership* 14, no. 3 (1956):

172–186.

"Hardwick History." Hardwick, VT Historical Society, October 17, 2023. https://hardwickvthistory.org/abouthardwick/hardwickhistory/.

Heifetz, Ronald. *Leadership Without Easy Answers*. Cambridge: Harvard University Press, 1998.

Heifetz, Ronald, Marty Linsky, and Alexander Grashow. *The Practice of Adaptive Leadership: Tools and Tactics for Changing Your Organization and the World*. Cambridge: Harvard Business Press, 2009.

Hersey, Paul, Kenneth Blanchard, and Dewey Johnson. *Management of Organizational Behavior: Leading Human Resources*. 10th ed. London: Pearson, 2012.

Horton, Adrian. "'They All Got On as One Family': The Story of a Woman Who Lived with Chimps." *Guardian*, April 29, 2021

https://www.theguardian.com/film/2021/apr/29/lucythehumanchimphbomax documentary.

Johnson, Spencer. *Who Moved My Cheese?* London: Vermillion, 1999.

Kabat-Zinn, Jon. *Mindfulness for Beginners: Reclaiming the Present Moment—and Your Life*. Louisville, CO: Sounds True, 2016.

Kaplan, Abraham. *The Conduct of Inquiry: Methodology for Behavioral Science*. New York: Routledge, 1973.

Knowles, Marc, and Sookyung Suh. "Performance System Analysis: Learning by Doing." *Performance Improvement* 44, no. 4 (2005): 35–42.

Kouzes, James, and Barry Posner. *The Leadership Challenge: How to Make Extraordinary Things Happen in Organizations*. 7th ed. San Francisco: Jossey-Bass, 2023.

Kruger, Justin, and David Dunning. "Unskilled and Unaware of It: How Difficulties in Recognizing One's Own Incompetence Lead to Inflated Self-Assessments." *Journal of Personality and Social Psychology* 77, no. 6 (1999): 1121-1134.

Lewin, Kurt, and Ronald Lippitt. "An Experimental Approach to the Study of Autocracy and Democracy: A Preliminary Note." *Sociometry* 1 (1938): 292–300.

Li, Roland. "Stanford Professor Says 5-Day Office Week Is Dead. But What's Replacing It?" San Francisco Chronicle, October 17, 2023. https://www.sfchronicle.com/projects//remoteworksurvey/.

Likert, Rensis. *New Patterns of Management*. New York: McGraw Hill, 1961.

Maslow, Abraham. "A Theory of Human Motivation." *Psychological Review* 50, no. 4 (1943): 370–396.

Maslow, Abraham. *Psychology of Science: A Reconnaissance*. Gateway Editions, 1969.

McGregor, Douglass. *The Human Side of Enterprise*. New York: McGraw Hill, 1960.

Miller, George. "The Magical Number Seven Plus or Minus Two: Some Limits on Our Capacity for Processing Information." *Psychological Review* 63, no. 2 (1956): 81–97.

Morgan, Jacob. *Leading with Vulnerability: Unlock Your Greatest Superpower to Transform Yourself, Your Team, and Your Organization*. Hoboken, NJ: Wiley, 2023.

Office of Student Support. "The Eisenhower Matrix." Columbia University School of Professional Studies, August 2023. https://sps.columbia.edu/sites/default/files/202308/Eisenhower%20Matrix.pdf.

Ouchi, William. *Theory Z: How American Business Can Meet the Japanese Challenge*. New York: Basic Books, 1981.

Pappas, Alexi. *Bravey: Chasing Dreams, Befriending Pain, and Other Big Ideas*. New York: The Dial Press, 2021.

Pearson, David, and Margaret Gallagher. "The Instruction of Reading Comprehension." *Contemporary Educational Psychology* 8, no. 3 (1983): 317–344.

Rogers, Carl. "A Theory of Therapy, Personality Relationships as Developed in the Client-Centered Framework." In *Psychology: A Study of a Science*, edited by Sigmund Koch. New York: McGraw Hill, 1959.

Rock, David, and Al Ringleb. *Handbook of Neuroleadership*. Independent Publisher, 2013.

Rosenman, Elizabeth, Jeremy Branzetti, and Rosemarie Fernandez. "Assessing Team Leadership in Emergency Medicine: The Milestones and Beyond." *Journal of Graduate Medical Education* 8, no. 3 (2016): 332–340.

Spector, Bert. "Carlyle, Freud, and the Great Man Theory More Fully Considered." *Leadership* 12, no. 2 (2015): 250–260.

Stogdill, Ralph. "Personal Factors Associated with Leadership: A Survey of the Literature." *Journal of Psychology* 25 (1948): 35–71.

Suzuki, Daisetz Teitaro. *Essays in Zen Buddhism (Third Series)*. New York: Samuel Weiser, 1934.

Sweller, John. "Cognitive Load During Problem-Solving: Effects on Learning." *Cognitive Science* 12, no. 2 (1988): 257–285.

Tannenbaum, Robert, and Warren Schmidt. "How to Choose a Leadership Pattern." *Harvard Business Review* 36 (1958): 95–101.

Tawwab, Nedra Glover. *Set Boundaries, Find Peace: A Guide to Reclaiming Yourself*. New York: Tarcher Perigee, 2021.

Tuckman, Bruce. "Development Sequence in Small Groups." *Psychological Bulletin* 63, no. 6 (1965): 384–399.

Tuckman, Bruce, and Mary Ann Jensen. "Stages of Small-Group Development Revisited." *Group and Organization Management* 2, no. 4 (1977): 419–427.

Van Valen, Leigh. "A New Evolutionary Law." *Evolutionary Theory* 1 (1973): 1–30.

Vygotsky, Lev. *Mind in Society: The Development of Higher Psychological Processes.* Cambridge: Harvard University Press, 1978.

Williams, Ted, and John Underwood. *The Science of Hitting.* New York: Simon & Schuster, 1986.

🍃 *We Grow Our Books in Montpelier, Vermont*

Learn more about our titles in Fiction, Nonfiction, Poetry and Children's Literature at the QR code below or visit www.rootstockpublishing.com.